THE PATH OF LOVE

By the same author

Unlocking the Gate of the Heart: Keys to Personal Transformation, A Bahá'í Approach

THE PATH
of
LOVE

by

Lasse Thoresen

GEORGE RONALD
OXFORD

George Ronald, *Publisher*
Oxford
www.grbooks.com

*A catalogue record for this book is available
from the British Library*

ISBN 0–85398–485–9

Printed and bound in Great Britain by
The Cromwell Press Ltd., Trowbridge, Wiltshire

CONTENTS

CONTENTS

*This is the Day whereon the Ocean of God's mercy
hath been manifested unto men, the Day in which
the Day Star of His loving-kindness hath shed its
radiance upon them, the Day in which the clouds of
His bountiful favour have overshadowed the whole
of mankind. Now is the time to cheer and refresh
the down-cast through the invigorating breeze of
love and fellowship, and the living waters of
friendliness and charity. . .*[1]

Bahá'u'lláh

PREFACE

To write a book on the subject of divine love may seem a strange thing to do, and I am the first to admit that practising divine love is far better and more important than writing about it. I started writing it because I realized that this was an aspect of life that I had not so far given sufficient attention to, and I wanted to improve my performance. So this book is not a scholarly dissertation on the subject, but rather a work destined to challenge habits of thought and feeling.

Fortunately, I am not alone in finding that writing and reading about this subject can be useful. Both Bahá'u'lláh, the Prophet-founder of the Bahá'í Faith, and 'Abdu'l-Bahá wrote hundreds, perhaps thousands, of pages expounding on the subject and encouraging us to action.

A couple of years before beginning this book, I wrote a book on meditation called *Unlocking the Gate of the Heart: Keys to Personal Transformation, A Bahá'í Approach*. The book dealt with a number of spiritual exercises that the Bahá'í Faith prescribes as necessary for the spiritual growth of all its practising adherents, and in addition many other proposals. However, having finished it, it seemed clear to me that I had not given sufficient attention to the importance of divine love. A closer scrutiny brought me to the conclusion that I myself had a very inadequate comprehension of this immense subject that has so many practical, spiritual, social, metaphysical and cosmological dimensions to it.

My main interest was in finding how to approach the subject in such a way that I could integrate it into my own thinking and feeling. I felt I needed to rehearse the new patterns of thought that seemed to emerge from the Bahá'í writings, thoughts that were very different from the ideas I formerly had on the subject.

I started to look for ways and means to rehearse these new thought patterns.

I have a musician's training, and rehearsing is a large part of any musician's life. When a master performer says "just do it like this, it is so simple" – yet the student does not manage to emulate the example – the master may have forgotten that what he now considers natural and simple actually came as a result of patient rehearsal and practice. Of course, the student with exceptional talent may need less rehearsal than the average student. However, most of us may be just average, and will profit from some rehearsing. And just as a perfectly mastered musical technique is valuable only when it demands no more attention so as to let the music through in a perfected form, so the exercises that this book leads up to aim at making of ourselves instruments of the spirit of love and unity.

In my quest for ways and means to rehearse divine love, I came across an article by Jordan and Margaret Paul, called "The Journey from Conflict to Love", published in *Lotus*, Fall 1991. Some ideas from this article have gone into Exercise 7 in Part 3 of the present book, an exercise that helps us to uncover the strategies employed by our lower, animal self when we feel threatened. The next thing I came upon was a major work on divine love, called *A Course in Miracles* (Foundation for Inner Peace, 1992). This book definitely influenced the way I organized the second and third parts of the present book. A few of the exercises proposed in Part 3 are based upon this course, but I have transferred the methods into the context of the Bahá'í Faith. In one of the exercises in Part 3, the attentive reader will also find traces of a spiritual exercise recommended by another Manifestion of God, namely Buddha in His Mahasattapathana Sutta.

The major part of this book, however, and its essence, is not what I have written, but the quotations from the Bahá'í writings – more than two hundred of them. It is these that deserve the main attention of the reader, for they condense a transcendent power that is capable of effecting a spiritual transformation in the reader's soul.

The disposition of the book now crystallized so that Part I deals with the subject of divine love in general, focusing on its transcendent origin, its distinctive character as opposed to other and more obvious forms of love, and the principle of the Holy Spirit, which it is necessary to practise in order to bring this almost superhuman form of love into reality.

Part II reiterates most of these subjects, but reformulates them as if the Spirit is addressing the reader. Instead of simply reading about the subject, the reader is now directly addressed and challenged in an "I – Thou" relationship.

Part III is for those who accept the challenge and at the same time decide to discipline themselves in order to master the practice of what for many will be novel perspectives on human relationships. Here the same subjects occur for the third time, but now in the form of specific exercises, which the reader may choose to carry out so as to train his mental habits and carry the essence of this book into practice.

This book would not have come into existence were it not for a number of willing helpers. My wife Britt Strandlie Thoresen contributed with ideas, discussions, patient support and inspiration, as well as by proofreading the original Norwegian edition. Ariane Schelderup rendered great assistance in organizing the quotations used. The Norwegian summer school committee, particularly Kari and Tore Skåtun, were helpful as consultation partners and in finding a venue to present the two first parts of the book. My daughter Sancra Thoresen provided the first translation of the material into English – prompted by an invitation by Hossein Danesh to present the book at the Landegg Academy. Part III was prepared in response to an invitation by Counsellor Larissa Tsutskova to come to Russia and hold a weekend retreat on this subject near Moscow.

Lasse Thoresen
Oslo, February 2004

PART I

THE QUALITIES OF LOVE

Hardly any topics are touched upon so often in the Bahá'í writings as those of love and unity. Love is the motive for the creation of the world; it is the only thing that can give a human being true and lasting joy, both in this world and in the next. Love is one in its essence, but expresses itself in innumerable ways throughout creation. The material world, although ultimately derived from God's love, is incapable of giving people any sort of lasting happiness or satisfaction; it is inconsistent and perishable and always lets down those who invest their love in it. Only by making the one, everlasting love the basis of life and action – divine love – can a human being find true joy, a joy that lasts forever. When this love becomes rooted in the heart, a person will be able to conduct himself or herself with happiness and safety in this world, and hence make the world a better place. This perishable world will become the arena for the practice of a love whose origin is not of it, but of an inexhaustible source we have found in our inner self, a source sustained and replenished by spiritual energies flowing from the universe's eternal centre of power, the transcendent Word of God.

To find this love is the most important thing a person can do in life. Everybody longs for peace and joy. But love exists in a myriad forms, and not every form of love leads us to the great, true love that bestows lasting peace and joy. Longing for true love can easily go astray and fail to obtain its goal.

The search for true love is difficult because the society we live in has an understanding of what love is that differs greatly from the one we find described in the Bahá'í writings. Naturally, our attitudes and emotions are shaped by our cultural background. If we are to come closer to the true, eternal love, it is therefore important that we are willing to subject our conventional and preconceived notions to a careful evaluation, combined with a willingness to adjust these in the light of the guidance gained from the Holy Writings. After all, none of us would wish to be prevented from attaining everlasting happiness by our fear of letting go of a perishable world. But this will demand of each of us that we earnestly and consciously accept the divinely inspired teachings that the Bahá'í writings offer on true happiness and love, and at the same time that we are willing to realize how illusory actually are the many idealized images of happiness and love with which society constantly indoctrinates us.

In Part I of this book we describe essential aspects of love and present related areas such as unity and the principle of the Holy Spirit.

DIVINE LOVE   1

Love is, in reality, the first effulgence of Divinity and the greatest splendour of God.[2]

'Abdu'l-Bahá

Love's creative power

Love was God's purpose in creating human beings:

O Son of Man! Veiled in My immemorial being and in the ancient eternity of My essence, I knew My love for thee; therefore I created thee, have engraved on thee Mine image and revealed to thee My beauty.[3]

Bahá'u'lláh

O Son of Man! I loved thy creation, hence I created thee. Wherefore, do thou love Me, that I may name thy name and fill thy soul with the spirit of life.[4]

Bahá'u'lláh

. . . love is the cause of the existence of all phenomena and . . . the absence of love is the cause of disintegration or nonexistence.[5]

'Abdu'l-Bahá

The purpose of God's creation is fulfilled when man responds with faith to the Creator's love:

I bear witness, O my God, that Thou hast created me to know Thee and to worship Thee.[6]

Bahá'u'lláh

I have breathed within thee a breath of My own Spirit, that thou mayest be My lover.[7]

Bahá'u'lláh

When a human being leaves the physical dimension, it will be able to return to the world of mercy that existed before either heaven or earth were created:

Grant him admission within the precincts of Thy transcendent mercy that was before the foundation of earth and heaven.[8]

Bahá'u'lláh

'Abdu'l-Bahá says that there are four kinds of love:

- God's love for God's own Self; God is love
- God's love for His children, His servants
- The human being's love for God
- Love between human beings

'Abdu'l-Bahá explains that even though divine love manifests itself in these four different ways, it still originates from God:

These four kinds of love originate from God. These are rays from the Sun of Reality; these are the Breathings of the Holy Spirit; these are the Signs of the Reality.[9]

'Abdu'l-Bahá

'Abdu'l-Bahá describes the four aspects of love as follows:

There are four kinds of love. The first is the love that flows from God to man; it consists of the inexhaustible graces, the Divine effulgence and heavenly illumination. Through this love the world of being receives life. Through this love man is endowed with physical existence, until, through the breath of the Holy Spirit – this same love – he receives eternal life and becomes the image of the Living God. This love is the origin of all the love in the world of creation.

The second is the love that flows from man to God. This is

faith, attraction to the Divine, enkindlement, progress, entrance into the Kingdom of God, receiving the Bounties of God, illumination with the lights of the Kingdom. This love is the origin of all philanthropy; this love causes the hearts of men to reflect the rays of the Sun of Reality.

The third is the love of God towards the Self or Identity of God. This is the transfiguration of His Beauty, the reflection of Himself in the mirror of His Creation. This is the reality of love, the Ancient Love, the Eternal Love. Through one ray of this Love all other love exists.

The fourth is the love of man for man. The love which exists between the hearts of believers is prompted by the ideal of the unity of spirits. This love is attained through the knowledge of God, so that men see the Divine Love reflected in the heart. Each sees in the other the Beauty of God reflected in the soul, and finding this point of similarity, they are attracted to one another in love. This love will make all men the waves of one sea, this love will make them all the stars of one heaven and the fruits of one tree. This love will bring the realization of true accord, the foundation of real unity.[10]

'Abdu'l-Bahá

Love is the essence of the Bahá'í Faith

Love is the mightiest power in the universe; this is why it is of pre-eminent importance in the Bahá'í teachings:

What a power is love! It is the most wonderful, the greatest of all living powers.

Love gives life to the lifeless. Love lights a flame in the heart that is cold. Love brings hope to the hopeless and gladdens the hearts of the sorrowful.

In the world of existence there is indeed no greater power than the power of love.[11]

'Abdu'l-Bahá

O ye loved ones of God! In this, the Bahá'í Dispensation, God's Cause is spirit unalloyed. His Cause belongeth not to the material world. It cometh neither for strife nor war, nor for acts of mischief or of shame; it is neither for quarrelling with other Faiths, nor for conflicts with the nations. Its only army is the love of God, its only joy the clear wine of His knowledge, its only battle the expounding of the Truth; its one crusade is against the insistent self, the evil promptings of the human heart. Its victory is to submit and yield, and to be selfless is its everlasting glory. In brief, it is spirit upon spirit . . .[12]

'Abdu'l-Bahá

Know thou of a certainty that Love is the secret of God's holy Dispensation, the manifestation of the All-Merciful, the fountain of spiritual outpourings.[13]

'Abdu'l-Bahá

The essence of Bahá'u'lláh's Teaching is all-embracing love, for love includeth every excellence of humankind. It causeth every soul to go forward. It bestoweth on each one, for a heritage, immortal life. Ere long shalt thou bear witness that His celestial Teachings, the very glory of reality itself, shall light up the skies of the world.[14]

'Abdu'l-Bahá

The message of love has also been of importance in earlier religions, but love and unity were often restricted to a certain group of people – such as those of the same tribe, the same race, the same nation, or those who belonged to the "only true faith". In the age of the Bahá'í Faith it is the universal aspect of divine love that is emphasized. This love is unlimited, not restricted to a particular group, for it is the Creator's own love for each and every one of His children.

In every dispensation, there hath been the commandment of fellowship and love, but it was a commandment limited to the community of those in mutual agreement, not to the dissident foe. In this wondrous age, however, praised be God, the commandments of God are not delimited, not restricted to any one group of people, rather have all the friends been commanded

6

to show forth fellowship and love, consideration and generosity and loving-kindness to every community on earth.[15]

'Abdu'l-Bahá

How the power of love reveals itself in the world

Love is heaven's kindly light, the Holy Spirit's eternal breath that vivifieth the human soul. Love is the cause of God's revelation unto man, the vital bond inherent, in accordance with the divine creation, in the realities of things. Love is the one means that ensureth true felicity both in this world and the next. Love is the light that guideth in darkness, the living link that uniteth God with man, that assureth the progress of every illumined soul. Love is the most great law that ruleth this mighty and heavenly cycle, the unique power that bindeth together the divers elements of this material world, the supreme magnetic force that directeth the movements of the spheres in the celestial realms. Love revealeth with unfailing and limitless power the mysteries latent in the universe. Love is the spirit of life unto the adorned body of mankind, the establisher of true civilization in this mortal world, and the shedder of imperishable glory upon every high-aiming race and nation.[16]

'Abdu'l-Bahá

The power holding everything together in the universe is love, and thus love makes possible the existence of everything. Without it we would all die, fall apart and disintegrate. This power holding things together is manifested in various ways at different levels of creation – from the mineral kingdom through the plant and animal kingdoms – and is expressed in the relationship between people. Love shows its true power in the spiritual Kingdom, since it is through love that human beings can take part in God's bounties and attain to life in the eternal worlds of God:

We declare that love is the cause of the existence of all phenomena and that the absence of love is the cause of disintegration or nonexistence. Love is the conscious bestowal of God, the bond of affiliation in all phenomena. We will first

7

consider the proof of this through sense perception. As we look upon the universe, we observe that all composite beings or existing phenomena are made up primarily of single elements bound together by a power of attraction. Through this power of attraction cohesion has become manifest between atoms of these composing elements. The resultant being is a phenomenon of the lower contingent type. The power of cohesion expressed in the mineral kingdom is in reality love or affinity manifested in a low degree according to the exigencies of the mineral world. We take a step higher into the vegetable kingdom where we find an increased power of attraction has become manifest among the composing elements which form phenomena. Through this degree of attraction a cellular admixture is produced among these elements which make up the body of a plant. Therefore, in the degree of the vegetable kingdom there is love. We enter the animal kingdom and find the attractive power binding together single elements as in the mineral, plus the cellular admixture as in the vegetable, plus the phenomena of feelings or susceptibilities. We observe that the animals are susceptible to certain affiliation and fellowship and that they exercise natural selection. This elemental attraction, this admixture and selective affinity is love manifest in the degree of the animal kingdom.

Finally, we come to the kingdom of man. As this is the superior kingdom, the light of love is more resplendent. In man we find the power of attraction among the elements which compose his material body, plus the attraction which produces cellular admixture or augmentative power, plus the attraction which characterizes the sensibilities of the animal kingdom, but still beyond and above all these lower powers we discover in the being of man the attraction of heart, the susceptibilities and affinities which bind men together, enabling them to live and associate in friendship and solidarity. It is, therefore, evident that in the world of humanity the greatest king and sovereign is love. If love were extinguished, the power of attraction dispelled, the affinity of human hearts destroyed, the phenomena of human life would disappear.

. . . But these are only degrees of love which exist in the natural

8

or physical world. Their manifestation is ever according to the requirement of natural conditions and standards.

Real love is the love which exists between God and His servants, the love which binds together holy souls. This is the love of the spiritual world, not the love of physical bodies and organisms. For example, consider and observe how the bestowals of God successively descend upon mankind, how the divine effulgences ever shine upon the human world. There can be no doubt that these bestowals, these bounties, these effulgences emanate from love. Unless love be the divine motive, it would be impossible for the heart of man to attain or receive them. Unless love exists, the divine blessing could not descend upon any object or thing. Unless there be love, the recipient of divine effulgence could not radiate and reflect that effulgence upon other objects. If we are of those who perceive, we realize that the bounties of God manifest themselves continuously, even as the rays of the sun unceasingly emanate from the solar centre. The phenomenal world through the resplendent effulgence of the sun is radiant and bright. In the same way the realm of hearts and spirits is illumined and resuscitated through the shining rays of the Sun of Reality and the bounties of the love of God. Thereby the world of existence, the kingdom of hearts and spirits, is ever quickened into life. Were it not for the love of God, hearts would be inanimate, spirits would wither, and the reality of man would be bereft of the everlasting bestowals.[17]

'Abdu'l-Bahá

The power behind true happiness is the love of God; a person who has attained this love has arrived in paradise whether he is living in this physical world or has passed on:

O Son of Being! Thy Paradise is My love; thy heavenly home, reunion with Me. Enter therein and tarry not. This is that which hath been destined for thee in Our kingdom above and Our exalted Dominion.[18]

Bahá'u'lláh

As to Paradise: It is a reality and there can be no doubt about it, and now in this world it is realized through love of Me and My good-pleasure. Whosoever attaineth unto it God will aid him in this world below, and after death He will enable him to gain admittance into Paradise whose vastness is as that of heaven and earth. Therein the Maids of glory and holiness will wait upon him in the daytime and in the night season, while the day-star of the unfading beauty of his Lord will at all times shed its radiance upon him and he will shine so brightly that no one shall bear to gaze at him.[19]

Bahá'u'lláh

Even though God's love includes everything, there exists a special bond between those souls who are on the same level of spiritual insight:

> The people of Bahá, who are the inmates of the Ark of God, are, one and all, well aware of one another's state and condition, and are united in the bonds of intimacy and fellowship. Such a state, however, must depend upon their faith and their conduct. They that are of the same grade and station are fully aware of one another's capacity, character, accomplishments and merits. They that are of a lower grade, however, are incapable of comprehending adequately the station, or of estimating the merits, of those that rank above them. Each shall receive his share from thy Lord. Blessed is the man that hath turned his face towards God, and walked steadfastly in His love, until his soul hath winged its flight unto God, the Sovereign Lord of all, the Most Powerful, the Ever-Forgiving, the All-Merciful.[20]

Bahá'u'lláh

Love of the world and love of God are mutually exclusive

The power of love has both material and spiritual expressions. While material forms of love are easier to observe and experience, the purpose of life is to obtain the spiritual form of love. Most people will agree that no great effort is required by a person to experience love in the form of gravity, which is the way planet

Earth expresses its love for us. Sexual love is another material expression of love which may be relatively simple to experience. Even the love of one's country or fellowship in common interests are material expressions of love. As with everything that is material, these are ephemeral and perishable; none of them can ensure lasting happiness, because the material world is always deceptive. The Bahá'í writings encourage us to be on our guard so that we do not mistake material forms of love for true love. True love does not originate in the material world; on the contrary, it comes from the "placeless Kingdom", the spiritual world. This love will give people lasting joy and real security; it is both the goal and the means for the spiritual development of individuals, and also for the interactions between them. It can only be achieved when one opens his heart to the influence and power of the Holy Spirit.

A strong emotional attachment to another person is not necessarily love. Infatuation or admiration may suddenly change; they lack the constancy inherent in divine love:

> But the love which sometimes exists between friends is not (true) love, because it is subject to transmutation; this is merely fascination. As the breeze blows, the slender trees yield. If the wind is in the East the tree leans to the West, and if the wind turns to the West the tree leans to the East. This kind of love is originated by the accidental conditions of life. This is not love, it is merely acquaintanceship; it is subject to change.
>
> Today you will see two souls apparently in close friendship; tomorrow all this may be changed. Yesterday they were ready to die for one another, today they shun one another's society! This is not love; it is the yielding of the hearts to the accidents of life. When that which has caused this "love" to exist passes, the love passes also; this is not in reality love.[21]
>
> 'Abdu'l-Bahá

In the West, passionate love for another person is often considered the highest form of love. Films, magazines and books all support the myth that a passionate relationship with an ideal partner will make a person happy. This obsession with passionate love causes adultery and divorce to flourish, as the dream to experience ever more passion and happiness restlessly changes its direction. In the Bahá'í writings, passionate love and attachment to another person are not considered capable of giving lasting happiness to anyone. On the contrary, the love of God is in the place of honour, and it is inseparable from allegiance towards the ethical principles which are revealed by Him whom we love above everything else:

> . . . we must reach a spiritual plane where God comes first and great human passions are unable to turn us away from Him. All the time we see people who either through the force of hate or the passionate attachment they have to another person, sacrifice principle or bar themselves from the path of God. . .
>
> We must love God, and in this state, a general love for all men becomes possible. We cannot love each human being for himself, but our feeling towards humanity should be motivated by our love for the Father who created all men.[22]
>
> *Written on behalf of Shoghi Effendi*

Divine love is unlimited. It is a power that the Creator allows to embrace all humankind, and thereby every individual. We must not be led to believe that the love we may feel for a restricted group of people can fully express this universal love. Most important, we should take care not to conduct ourselves with hatred, despite, condescension or indifference towards people who do not belong to the same group as we do.

> In order that love may manifest its power there must be an object, an instrument, a motive.
>
> There are many ways of expressing the love principle; there is love for the family, for the country, for the race, there is political enthusiasm, there is also the love of community of interest in service. These are all ways and means of showing the power of love. Without any such means, love would be unseen, unheard, unfelt – altogether unexpressed, unmanifested! . . . So, it is necessary to have an instrument, a motive for love's manifestation, an object, a mode of expression.

We must find a way of spreading love among the sons of humanity.

Love is unlimited, boundless, infinite! Material things are limited, circumscribed, finite. You cannot adequately express infinite love by limited means.

The perfect love needs an unselfish instrument, absolutely freed from fetters of every kind. The love of family is limited; the tie of blood relationship is not the strongest bond. Frequently members of the same family disagree, and even hate each other.

Patriotic love is finite . . .

The love of race is limited . . .

Political love also is much bound up with hatred of one party for another . . .

The love of community of interest in service is likewise fluctuating . . .

The great unselfish love for humanity is bounded by none of these imperfect, semi-selfish bonds; this is the one perfect love, possible to all mankind, and can only be achieved by the power of the Divine Spirit. No worldly power can accomplish the universal love.

Let all be united in this Divine power of love! Let all strive to grow in the light of the Sun of Truth, and reflecting this luminous love on all men, may their hearts become so united that they may dwell evermore in the radiance of the limitless love . . .

When you love a member of your family or a compatriot, let it be with a ray of the Infinite Love! Let it be in God, and for God! Wherever you find the attributes of God love that person, whether he be of your family or of another. Shed the light of a boundless love on every human being whom you meet, whether of your country, your race, your political party, or of any other nation, colour or shade of political opinion. Heaven will support you while you work in this in-gathering of the scattered peoples of the world beneath the shadow of the almighty tent of unity.

You will be servants of God, who are dwelling near to Him, His divine helpers in the service, ministering to all Humanity. *All* Humanity! Every human being! *never forget this!*[23]

'Abdu'l-Bahá

Spiritual love does not have its origin in the physical body – which implies, among other things, that it is not dependent on the different emotions and moods of the body. Although spiritual love originates in the spiritual world, this does not mean that under the right circumstances it cannot be felt by the physical body. The human body is a tool for expressing divine love in different ways, such as serving others and coming closer to God:

> For love of God and spiritual attraction do cleanse and purify the human heart and dress and adorn it with the spotless garment of holiness; and once the heart is entirely attached to the Lord, and bound over to the Blessed Perfection, then will the grace of God be revealed.
>
> This love is not of the body but completely of the soul . . .
>
> Wherefore must the friends of God, with utter sanctity, with one accord, rise up in the spirit, in unity with one another, to such a degree that they will become even as one being and one soul. On such a plane as this, physical bodies play no part, rather doth the spirit take over and rule; and when its power encompasseth all then is spiritual union achieved. Strive ye by day and night to cultivate your unity to the fullest degree. Let your thoughts dwell on your own spiritual development, and close your eyes to the deficiencies of other souls. Act ye in such wise, showing forth pure and goodly deeds, and modesty and humility, that ye will cause others to be awakened.[24]
>
> *'Abdu'l-Bahá*

Material expressions of love always have a touch of egoism to them, and may easily become unfortunate substitutions for true love. Since a human being has only one heart, there is only one residence where love can dwell. As long as material love rules the heart, spiritual love is excluded. Divine love must have the seat of honour in the heart; all other forms of love must be subordinate to this one love. One beam of divine love will be able to illumine and give meaning to all other, more limited forms of love, if we only dare to let go of attachment to the world of these forms and attributes, and let the Spirit of God take the seat of honour in our hearts.

To detach oneself from love of the world is a process requiring some discipline. Practising the moral laws of the Bahá'í Faith will give us this. It also requires willingness to see the value of critical or painful situations. Hence, divine love presupposes our detachment from other kinds of love:

> Return, then, and cleave wholly unto God, and cleanse thine heart from the world and all its vanities, and suffer not the love of any stranger to enter and dwell therein. Not until thou dost purify thine heart from every trace of such love can the brightness of the light of God shed its radiance upon it, for to none hath God given more than one heart. This, verily, hath been decreed and written down in His ancient Book. And as the human heart, as fashioned by God, is one and undivided, it behoveth thee to take heed that its affections be, also, one and undivided. Cleave thou, therefore, with the whole affection of thine heart, unto His love, and withdraw it from the love of anyone besides Him, that He may aid thee to immerse thyself in the ocean of His unity, and enable thee to become a true upholder of His oneness. God is My witness. My sole purpose in revealing to thee these words is to sanctify thee from the transitory things of the earth, and aid thee to enter the realm of everlasting glory, that thou mayest, by the leave of God, be of them that abide and rule therein . . .[25]
>
> *Bahá'u'lláh*

The process of detachment is synonymous with learning to control our ego, our lower self, and to make it subordinate to our higher self.

> The ego is the animal in us, the heritage of the flesh which is full of *selfish* desires. By obeying the laws of God, seeking to live the life laid down in our teachings, and prayer and struggle, we can subdue our egos. We call people "Saints" who have achieved the highest degree of mastery over their ego.[26]
>
> *Written on behalf of Shoghi Effendi*

Love is Alpha and Omega, beginning and end. When divine love is in the seat of honour, whatever we do will be of service for ourselves and others, while without this everything will be harmful. Intellectual knowledge, studies and the use of scientific principles will only be of use to people when placed in the context of universal love, and when they take into consideration what serves humanity best:

O thou son of the Kingdom! All things are beneficial if joined with the love of God; and without His love all things are harmful, and act as a veil between man and the Lord of the Kingdom. When His love is there, every bitterness turneth sweet, and every bounty rendereth a wholesome pleasure. For example, a melody, sweet to the ear, bringeth the very spirit of life to a heart in love with God, yet staineth with lust a soul engrossed in sensual desires. And every branch of learning, conjoined with the love of God, is approved and worthy of praise; but bereft of His love, learning is barren – indeed, it bringeth on madness. Every kind of knowledge, every science, is as a tree: if the fruit of it be the love of God, then is it a blessed tree, but if not, that tree is but dried-up wood, and shall only feed the fire.[27]

'Abdu'l-Bahá

THE PRINCIPLE OF UNITY 2

Humankind is one

The age has dawned when human fellowship will become a reality.

The century has come when all religions shall be unified.

The dispensation is at hand when all nations shall enjoy the blessings of international peace.

The cycle has arrived when racial prejudice will be abandoned by tribes and peoples of the world.

The epoch has begun wherein all native lands will be conjoined in one great human family.

For all mankind shall dwell in peace and security beneath the shelter of the great tabernacle of the one living God.[28]

'Abdu'l-Bahá

The oneness of mankind is a central principle in the Bahá'í Faith. Humankind is one because we all come from one Creator. We have a natural tendency to see ourselves and the people we know as separate, unique or special. In the writings of the Bahá'í Faith it is first of all emphasized that the whole of humanity is one great organism animated by a common spiritual reality. This spiritual reality is one and has always been one. The time for this spiritual, unchangeable unity to be expressed in the material world has now arrived. This implies that humankind will develop global institutions that coordinate relations between people and nations, institutions that secure justice and peace in the global community. The global community on our planet will be the reflection in the physical world of a higher spiritual reality. This animating and unifying force is the common spiritual reality of

God's messengers throughout the ages, such as Moses, Christ, Muḥammad, Krishna, Buddha and Bahá'u'lláh:

> For all parts of the creational world are of one whole. Christ the Manifestor reflecting the divine Sun represented the whole. All the parts are subordinate and obedient to the whole. The contingent beings are the branches of the tree of life while the Messenger of God is the root of that tree. The branches, leaves and fruit are dependent for their existence upon the root of the tree of life.[29]
>
> 'Abdu'l-Bahá

> Just as the human spirit of life is the cause of coordination among the various parts of the human organism, the Holy Spirit is the controlling cause of the unity and coordination of mankind. That is to say, the bond or oneness of humanity cannot be effectively established save through the power of the Holy Spirit, for the world of humanity is a composite body, and the Holy Spirit is the animating principle of its life.[30]
>
> 'Abdu'l-Bahá

The Bahá'í writings compare humankind with the branches of a tree. For 'Abdu'l-Bahá, this seems to be more than just a poetic simile. It is rather an insight into how reality is actually constituted, an insight leading to a different attitude towards others, a different way of acting:

> The Blessed Beauty saith: "Ye are all the fruits of one tree, the leaves of one branch." Thus hath He likened this world of being to a single tree, and all its peoples to the leaves thereof, and the blossoms and fruits. It is needful for the bough to blossom, and leaf and fruit to flourish, and upon the interconnection of all parts of the world-tree, dependeth the flourishing of leaf and blossom, and the sweetness of the fruit.
>
> For this reason must all human beings powerfully sustain one another and seek for everlasting life; and for this reason must the lovers of God in this contingent world become the mercies and the blessings sent forth by that clement King of the seen and

unseen realms. Let them purify their sight and behold all humankind as leaves and blossoms and fruits of the tree of being. Let them at all times concern themselves with doing a kindly thing for one of their fellows, offering to someone love, consideration, thoughtful help. Let them see no one as their enemy, or as wishing them ill, but think of all humankind as their friends; regarding the alien as an intimate, the stranger as a companion, staying free of prejudice, drawing no lines.[31]

'Abdu'l-Bahá

In this passage 'Abdu'l-Bahá shows us that from the acknowledgement of the organic unity of all people follows the realization that no one can actually be a complete stranger, nobody can be regarded as entirely hostile or unwelcome. We must let all dividing lines fall, and stop categorizing and judging others. If we seriously regard all as one, then judging others will become synonymous with judging ourselves, attacking others the same as attacking ourselves, viewing others as strangers equal to alienating ourselves. If, on the contrary, we serve others and seek to find God therein, we will come closer to our own selves, which is identical with coming closer to God.

Today the confirmations of the Kingdom of Abhá are with those who renounce themselves, forget their own opinions, cast aside personalities and are thinking of the welfare of others . . . Whosoever is occupied with himself is wandering in the desert of heedlessness and regret. The "Master Key" to self-mastery is self forgetting. The road to the palace of life is through the path of renunciation.[32]

The more we search for ourselves, the less likely we are to find ourselves; and the more we search for God, and to serve our fellow-men, the more profoundly will we become acquainted with ourselves, and the more inwardly assured. This is one of the great spiritual laws of life.[33]

Written on behalf of Shoghi Effendi

'Abdu'l-Bahá's spiritual sight was so well developed that He was able to see the spiritual reality uniting people. Once, when He was before a gathering of people, He expressed it as follows:

> If you could see with the eye of truth, great waves of spirituality would be visible to you in this place. The power of the Holy Spirit is here for all. Praise be to God that your hearts are inspired with Divine fervour! Your souls are as waves on the sea of the spirit; although each individual is a distinct wave, the ocean is one, all are united in God.
>
> Every heart should radiate unity, so that the Light of the one Divine Source of all may shine forth bright and luminous. We must not consider the separate waves alone, but the entire sea. We should rise from the individual to the whole. The spirit is as one great ocean and the waves thereof are the souls of men.[34]
>
> *'Abdu'l-Bahá*

The Bahá'í Faith represents a new Covenant between God and humanity. Through His "interference" in history, God has changed the relationships between human beings and introduced an era when world peace is destined to become a reality. Fundamental to this new orientation in the history of humankind is the removal of the idea of the "great enemy" from religion. This took place in the mystical intercourse between God and Bahá'u'lláh as the representative of all mankind, when during the days of Riḍván all things were "immersed in the sea of purification":

> Verily, all created things were immersed in the sea of purification when, on that first day of Riḍván, We shed upon the whole of creation the splendours of Our most excellent Names and Our most exalted Attributes. This, verily, is a token of My loving providence, which hath encompassed all the worlds. Consort ye then with the followers of all religions, and proclaim ye the Cause of your Lord, the Most Compassionate; this is the very crown of deeds, if ye be of them who understand.[35]
>
> *Bahá'u'lláh*

In the Bahá'í teachings certain races or nations are no longer singled out as being superior to others, nor is any people, religion or ethnic group called the "people of Satan". What we usually call "evil" is characterized by 'Abdu'l-Bahá as weakness that calls for loving attention rather than damnation. God has created every individual, and being the Creator, He naturally loves and cares about His creation. We have to make this perspective our own, and base our thoughts and actions on this universal perspective, rather than on our own limited point of view:

> Consider what injuries, ordeals and calamities have been inflicted upon mankind since the beginning of history. Every city, country, nation and people has been subjected to the destruction and havoc of war. Each one of the divine religions considers itself as belonging to a goodly and blessed tree, the tree of the Merciful, and all other religious systems as belonging to a tree of evil, the tree of Satan. For this reason they heap execration and abuse upon each other . . .
>
> When the light of Bahá'u'lláh dawned from the East, He proclaimed the promise of the oneness of humanity. He addressed all mankind, saying, "Ye are all the fruits of one tree. There are not two trees: one a tree of divine mercy, the other the tree of Satan." Again He said, "Ye are all the fruits of one tree, the leaves of one branch." This was His announcement; this was His promise of the oneness of the world of humanity. Anathema and execration were utterly abrogated. He said, "It is not becoming in man to curse another; it is not befitting that man should attribute darkness to another; it is not meet that one human being should consider another human being as bad; nay, rather, all mankind are the servants of one God; God is the Father of all; there is not a single exception to that law. There are no people of Satan; all belong to the Merciful. There is no darkness; all is light. All are the servants of God, and man must love humanity from his heart. He must, verily, behold humanity as submerged in the divine mercy."
>
> Bahá'u'lláh has made no exception to this rule. He said that among mankind there may be those who are ignorant; they must be trained. Some are sick; they must be treated. Some are immature; they must be helped to attain maturity. In other respects humanity is submerged in the ocean of divine mercy.

God is the Father of all. He educates, provides for and loves all; for they are His servants and His creation. Surely the Creator loves His creatures. It would be impossible to find an artist who does not love his own production. Have you ever seen a man who did not love his own actions? Even though they be bad actions, he loves them. How ignorant, therefore, the thought that God, Who created man, educated and nurtured him, surrounded him with all blessings, made the sun and all phenomenal existence for his benefit, bestowed upon him tenderness and kindness and then did not love him. This is palpable ignorance, for no matter to what religion a man belongs, even though he be an atheist or materialist, nevertheless, God nurtures him, bestows His kindness and sheds upon him His light. How then can we believe God is wrathful and unloving? How can we even imagine this, when as a matter of fact we are witnesses of the tenderness and mercy of God upon every hand? All about us we behold manifestations of the love of God. If, therefore, God be loving, what should we do? We have nothing else to do but to emulate Him. Just as God loves all and is kind to all, so must we really love and be kind to everybody. We must consider none bad, none worthy of detestation, no one as an enemy. We must love all; nay, we must consider everyone as related to us, for all are the servants of one God. All are under the instructions of one Educator. We must strive day and night that love and amity may increase, that this bond of unity may be strengthened, that joy and happiness may more and more prevail, that in unity and solidarity all mankind may gather beneath the shadow of God, that people may turn to God for their sustenance, finding in Him the life that is everlasting. Thus may they be confirmed in the Kingdom of God and live forever through His grace and bounty.[36]

'Abdu'l-Bahá

People always have a tendency to draw dividing lines by paying extra attention to the characteristics that separate them from others, and by doing so declaring themselves or their group to be the best. This sort of thinking makes limitations and differences the most important factor: establishing a unity becomes identical with marking out differences in relation to another group. The

Bahá'í writings, on the contrary, underline the type of unity that has no contradictions, a limitless unity including all that is:

What is real unity? When we observe the human world, we find various collective expressions of unity therein. For instance, man is distinguished from the animal by his degree, or kingdom. This comprehensive distinction includes all the posterity of Adam and constitutes one great household or human family, which may be considered the fundamental or physical unity of mankind. Furthermore, a distinction exists between various groups of humankind according to lineage, each group forming a racial unity separate from the others. There is also the unity of tongue among those who use the same language as a means of communication; national unity where various peoples live under one form of government such as French, German, British, etc.; and political unity, which conserves the civil rights of parties or factions of the same government. All these unities are imaginary and without real foundation, for no real result proceeds from them. The purpose of true unity is real and divine outcomes. From these limited unities mentioned only limited outcomes proceed, whereas unlimited unity produces unlimited result. For instance, from the limited unity of race or nationality the results at most are limited. It is like a family living alone and solitary; there are no unlimited or universal outcomes from it.

The unity which is productive of unlimited results is first a unity of mankind which recognizes that all are sheltered beneath the overshadowing glory of the All-Glorious, that all are servants of one God; for all breathe the same atmosphere, live upon the same earth, move beneath the same heavens, receive effulgence from the same sun and are under the protection of one God. This is the most great unity, and its results are lasting if humanity adheres to it; but mankind has hitherto violated it, adhering to sectarian or other limited unities such as racial, patriotic or unity of self-interests; therefore, no great results have been forthcoming. Nevertheless, it is certain that the radiance and favours of God are encompassing, minds have developed, perceptions have become acute, sciences and arts are widespread, and capacity exists for the proclamation and promulgation of the real and ultimate unity of mankind, which will bring forth marvellous results. It will reconcile all religions, make warring nations loving, cause hostile kings to become friendly and bring peace and happiness to the human world. It will cement together the Orient and Occident, remove forever the foundations of war and upraise the ensign of the Most Great Peace.[37]

'Abdu'l-Bahá

In order to be able to see people in this way, it is necessary to develop willingness and ability to overlook all the things in other people that we would regard as mistakes and limitations. It is clear that all that is earthly has limitations and may hence be criticized from another, also limited, point of view. But such a limited way of looking at human beings can only strengthen a materialistic perspective, both in ourselves and others. God, on the other hand, encourages us to view people in the light of the perfection in which He created the whole of humanity.

God is great! God is kind! He does not behold human shortcomings; He does not regard human weaknesses. Man is a creature of His mercy, and to His mercy He summons all. Why then should we despise or detest His creatures because this one is a Jew, another a Buddhist or Zoroastrian and so on? This is ignorance, for the oneness of humanity as servants of God is an assured and certain fact.[38]

'Abdu'l-Bahá

The basis for understanding this true brotherhood between all the peoples of the world lies in the inspiration given by a living spiritual power: the Holy Spirit. It is this Spirit that teaches us to view each other in a different light, the light of unity. Without this power and inspiration, there would be no possibility for any human being to sincerely understand the truth and reality of the unity of humankind.

It is evident, therefore, that the foundation of real brotherhood, the cause of loving cooperation and reciprocity and the source of real kindness and unselfish devotion is none other than the breaths of the Holy Spirit. Without this influence and animus it is impossible. We may be able to realize some degrees of fraternity through other motives, but these are limited associations and subject to change. When human brotherhood is founded upon the Holy Spirit, it is eternal, changeless, unlimited.[39]

'Abdu'l-Bahá

One might ask if this universal perspective on love means that we are supposed to let all kinds of grave injustices go on – that we should just forgive it all. There is, however, nothing in the Bahá'í writings to suggest that the practising of divine love is incompatible with justice or that it leads to some kind of ethical *laissez-faire*. Divine love and divine justice are compatible and complement each other. The challenge is to sort out these two great spiritual principles in the right way. To do so, we have to look into the distinction between justice and revenge. Both of them lead to punishment, but the motive is different. The motive for justice is not hate or revenge, but a desire to uphold a civilized code of behaviour in society for the benefit of all. In the present state of the development of human civilization, there are institutions designed to mete out and execute justice, such as the courts and the police. This should leave individuals free of the responsibility to correct grave breaches of law and order personally. Instead, in our individual lives we are responsible for practising love and forgiveness, for focusing our attention on the good sides of another human being, however depraved and abject he may be.

If a criminal, having received his just punishment from an institution, is not regarded as fully human, if he is not forgiven by the community around him, how can he ever come back to begin a new and better life in dignity and self-respect? We shall return to this question of justice and mercy later in the book.

The consciousness of unity: a different way of seeing the world

The unity of humankind is thus a spiritual reality, and an important step in a person's spiritual development is not just knowing about it, but experiencing this reality. Bahá'u'lláh describes this experience in the following way:

> In this station [i.e. the Valley of Unity] he pierceth the veils of plurality, fleeth from the worlds of the flesh, and ascendeth into the heaven of singleness. With the ear of God he heareth, with the eye of God he beholdeth the mysteries of divine creation. He steppeth into the sanctuary of the Friend, and shareth as an intimate the pavilion of the Loved One. He stretcheth out the hand of truth from the sleeve of the Absolute; he revealeth the secrets of power. He seeth in himself neither name nor fame nor rank, but findeth his own praise in praising God. He beholdeth in his own name the name of God; to him, "all songs are from the King" and every melody from Him. He sitteth on the throne of "Say, all is from God," [Qur'án 4:80] and taketh his rest on the carpet of "There is no power or might but in God". [Qur'án 18:37]. He looketh on all things with the eye of oneness, and seeth the brilliant rays of the divine sun shining from the dawning-point of Essence alike on all created things, and the lights of singleness reflected over all creation . . .
>
> Whensoever the Splendour of the King of Oneness settleth upon the throne of the heart and soul, His shining becometh visible in every limb and member. At that time the mystery of the famed tradition gleameth out of darkness: "A servant is drawn unto Me in prayer until I answer him; and when I have answered him, I become the ear wherewith he heareth . . ." . . . the action and effect of the light are from the Light-Giver; so it is that all move through Him and arise by His will . . .[40]
>
> *Bahá'u'lláh*

The world will seem quite different to a person who has opened himself to this consciousness of unity. But of course, it is not the world that is different, it is the way we look at it that has changed. Spiritual development demands first of all that we learn to see the world in a different way – receiving new eyes and new ears. God has given every one of us the opportunity to experience the world from this perspective of unity; it is an ability latent within us all. And through His revelation, God has given us the guidance as to how we can develop these qualities.

When Bahá'u'lláh explains the consciousness of unity, He uses sunlight as an image. When sunlight shines on various objects, the beholder will experience different colours. Without the light there would be no experience of colour at all. But sunlight itself is always one, and in this image may therefore represent the unity in all that is. If we turn our gaze towards the object itself, we will experience differences, but if we look at the light and its source, the sun, we will experience unity. Without light, the power of unity, it would not even be possible to experience the differences between objects. Hence the light, the unity, is more fundamental than all the differences. To focus on the differences is like seeing the world with our ego as the point of reference; in this case we will only be capable of seeing a world where desire and conflict rule. To look towards the light is to see God in everything, and is a point of view that has its spring, its source, in our higher, spiritual self. When we view the world in this way we will always be conscious that without light there would not be a world to be seen at all. The aim of human life, then, is to develop a pure heart where God's light may shine clearly and from there reflect its light further on, into the world. This requires willingness to open and turn the mirror of our heart towards the lights of heaven, the light of unity, and away from the colours in a speckled world.

It is clear to thine Eminence that all the variations which the wayfarer in the stages of his journey beholdeth in the realms of being, proceed from his own vision. We shall give an example of this, that its meaning may become fully clear: Consider the visible sun; although it shineth with one radiance upon all things, and at the behest of the King of Manifestation bestoweth light on all creation, yet in each place it becometh manifest and sheddeth its bounty according to the potentialities of that place. For instance, in a mirror it reflecteth its own disk and shape, and this is due to the sensitivity of the mirror; in a crystal it maketh fire to appear, and in other things it showeth only the effect of its shining, but not its full disk. And yet, through that effect, by the command of the Creator, it traineth each thing according to the quality of that thing, as thou observest.

In like manner, colours become visible in every object according to the nature of that object. For instance, in a yellow globe, the rays shine yellow; in a white the rays are white; in a red, the red rays are manifest. Then these variations are from the object, not from the shining light. And if a place be shut away from the light, as by walls or a roof, it will be entirely bereft of the splendour of the light, nor will the sun shine thereon.

Thus it is that certain invalid souls have confined the lands of knowledge within the wall of self and passion, and clouded them with ignorance and blindness, and have been veiled from the light of the mystic sun and the mysteries of the Eternal Beloved . . .

In sum, the differences in objects have now been made plain. Thus when the wayfarer gazeth only upon the place of appearance – that is, when he seeth only the many-coloured globes – he beholdeth yellow and red and white; hence it is that conflict hath prevailed among the creatures, and a darksome dust from limited souls hath hid the world. And some do gaze upon the effulgence of the light; and some have drunk of the wine of oneness and these see nothing but the sun itself . . .

O My Brother! A pure heart is as a mirror; cleanse it with the burnish of love and severance from all save God, that the true sun may shine within it and the eternal morning dawn.[41]

Bahá'u'lláh

Truth is one

Humankind is one because truth is one. If all people seek the utmost truth, a unity between all people will be created. The differences between people are illusory when seen in the light of the great truth. To free ourselves from prejudice and sincerely seek the truth therefore becomes essential for the achievement of unity.

Being one, truth cannot be divided, and the differences that appear to exist among the nations only result from their attachment to prejudice. If only men would search out truth, they would find themselves united.[42]

'Abdu'l-Bahá

Truth is the same as reality. That which is true has a reality which is incorruptible and everlasting. God's Holy Manifestations, His Messengers, have guided people to this reality, which is the only solid foundation for peace and unity in the world:

> I hope that the lights of the Sun of Reality will illumine the whole world so that no strife and warfare, no battles and bloodshed remain. May fanaticism and religious bigotry be unknown, all humanity enter the bond of brotherhood, souls consort in perfect agreement, the nations of earth at last hoist the banner of truth, and the religions of the world enter the divine temple of oneness, for the foundations of the heavenly religions are one reality. Reality is not divisible; it does not admit multiplicity. All the holy Manifestations of God have proclaimed and promulgated the same reality. They have summoned mankind to reality itself, and reality is one.[43]

> *'Abdu'l-Bahá*

THE PRINCIPLE OF THE HOLY SPIRIT 3

It is evident, therefore, that the foundation of real brotherhood, the cause of loving cooperation and reciprocity and the source of real kindness and unselfish devotion is none other than the breaths of the Holy Spirit. Without this influence and animus it is impossible. We may be able to realize some degrees of fraternity through other motives, but these are limited associations and subject to change. When human brotherhood is founded upon the Holy Spirit, it is eternal, changeless, unlimited.[44]

'Abdu'l-Bahá

Just as the human spirit of life is the cause of coordination among the various parts of the human organism, the Holy Spirit is the controlling cause of the unity and coordination of mankind. That is to say, the bond or oneness of humanity cannot be effectively established save through the power of the Holy Spirit, for the world of humanity is a composite body, and the Holy Spirit is the animating principle of its life.[45]

'Abdu'l-Bahá

True unity, as the Bahá'í writings see it, cannot be achieved except through the power of the Holy Spirit. The Holy Spirit is the power connecting God with human beings. It is the power animating the Manifestations of God, bestowing upon them knowledge about matters they have not perceived through material organs. However, the power of the Holy Spirit is not restricted to God's Manifestations; it can inspire and help all who call upon it.

When 'Abdu'l-Bahá expounded the fundamental Bahá'í principles in Paris, He designated the principle of the Holy Spirit as one of them. He explains it as follows:

> In the teaching of Bahá'u'lláh, it is written: "By the Power of the Holy Spirit alone is man able to progress, for the power of man is limited and the Divine Power is boundless" . . .
>
> The Prophets of God have not all graduated in the schools of learned philosophy; indeed they were often men of humble birth, to all appearance ignorant, unknown men of no importance in the eyes of the world; sometimes even lacking the knowledge of reading and writing.
>
> That which raised these great ones above men, and by which they were able to become Teachers of the truth, was the power of the Holy Spirit. Their influence on humanity, by virtue of this mighty inspiration, was great and penetrating.
>
> The influence of the wisest philosophers, without this Spirit Divine, has been comparatively unimportant, however extensive their learning and deep their scholarship . . .
>
> An humble man without learning, but filled with the Holy Spirit, is more powerful than the most nobly-born profound scholar without that inspiration. He who is educated by the Divine Spirit can, in his time, lead others to receive the same Spirit.
>
> I pray for you that you may be informed by the life of the Divine Spirit, so that you may be the means of educating others. The life and morals of a spiritual man are, in themselves, an education to those who know him.
>
> Think not of your own limitations, dwell only on the welfare of the Kingdom of Glory. Consider the influence of Jesus Christ on His apostles, then think of their effect upon the world. These simple men were enabled by the power of the Holy Spirit to spread the glad tidings!
>
> So may you all receive Divine assistance! No capacity is limited when led by the Spirit of God![46]
>
> 'Abdu'l-Bahá

The principle of the Holy Spirit is this, then: that while the material human being has limited knowledge, love and willpower, he has access to a spiritual power which compensates for this, provided that the person acknowledges his limits and declares his faith in this power. When a person has acknowledged his limitations, he must forget these and rely utterly on the Holy Spirit to enable him to fulfil God's will. When the Holy Spirit so desires, it will illumine his mind and heart with its knowledge and love, and in this way let his heart become a channel for the spirit of God:

> Remember not your own limitations; the help of God will come to you. Forget yourself. God's help will surely come!
>
> When you call on the Mercy of God waiting to reinforce you, your strength will be tenfold.
>
> . . . One must never consider one's own feebleness, it is the strength of the Holy Spirit of Love, which gives the power to teach. The thought of our own weakness could only bring despair. We must look higher than all earthly thoughts; detach ourselves from every material idea, crave for the things of the spirit; fix our eyes on the everlasting bountiful Mercy of the Almighty, who will fill our souls with the gladness of joyful service to His command "Love One Another".[47]
>
> 'Abdu'l-Bahá

The Holy Spirit is a force that makes human beings capable of conquering the limitations inherent in their nature. It assists human beings to make discoveries enabling them to overcome some of nature's limitations in the material world. Similarly, it helps human beings to overcome their personal limitations when it comes to being a channel for the eternal, divine love:

> The power of the Holy Spirit, enlightening man's intelligence, has enabled him to discover means of bending many natural laws to his will. He flies through the air, floats on the sea, and even moves under the waters.
>
> All this proves how man's intelligence has been enabled to free him from the limitations of nature, and to solve many of her mysteries. Man, to a certain extent, has broken the chains of matter.

The Holy Spirit will give to man greater powers than these, if only he will strive after the things of the spirit and endeavour to attune his heart to the Divine infinite love.[48]

'Abdu'l-Bahá

. . . the Lord of mankind has caused His holy, divine Manifestations to come into the world. He has revealed His heavenly Books in order to establish spiritual brotherhood and through the power of the Holy Spirit has made it practicable for perfect fraternity to be realized among mankind. And when through the breaths of the Holy Spirit this perfect fraternity and agreement are established amongst men – this brotherhood and love being spiritual in character, this loving-kindness being heavenly, these constraining bonds being divine – a unity appears which is indissoluble, unchanging and never subject to transformation. It is ever the same and will forever remain the same.[49]

'Abdu'l-Bahá

The power of love which created the world reappears within the world to guide the people back to this primeval love. The Holy Spirit has the role of intermediary: it is like the beams of sunlight that mediate between the sun and the earth. The first receivers of the rays of the Sun of God in this created world are God's Manifestations. They function as perfect mirrors reflecting light onto the whole of humanity. Through their revelations the Holy Spirit's universal power of love is transformed into particular utterances in a human language.

To lay the foundations for loving relationships between people has always been a purpose of the Manifestations of God. By coming into contact with the spirit of God's Manifestations, every individual may be filled with the spirit of love and become a channel of divine love to others.

For a single purpose were the Prophets, each and all, sent down to earth; for this was Christ made manifest, for this did Bahá'u'lláh raise up the call of the Lord: that the world of man should become the world of God, this nether realm the Kingdom, this darkness light, this satanic wickedness all the virtues of heaven – and unity, fellowship and love be won for the whole human race, that the organic unity should reappear and the bases of discord be destroyed and life everlasting and grace everlasting become the harvest of mankind.[50]

'Abdu'l-Bahá

The advent of the prophets and the revelation of the Holy Books is intended to create love between souls and friendship between the inhabitants of the earth. Real love is impossible unless one turn his face towards God and be attracted to His Beauty.[51]

'Abdu'l-Bahá

To be able to give this gift of love to people, the Manifestations of God have endured immeasurable suffering. Christ was crucified, the Báb was imprisoned and executed, and Bahá'u'lláh suffered the worst tests in numerous prisons and through various forms of persecution. But they never wavered, and so became living evidence of the great power of love which it was the purpose of their lives to share with us:

Consider to what extent the love of God makes itself manifest. Among the signs of His love which appear in the world are the dawning points of His Manifestations. What an infinite degree of love is reflected by the divine Manifestations toward mankind! For the sake of guiding the people They have willingly forfeited Their lives to resuscitate human hearts. They have accepted the cross. To enable human souls to attain the supreme degree of advancement, They have suffered during Their limited years extreme ordeals and difficulties. If Jesus Christ had not possessed love for the world of humanity, surely He would not have welcomed the cross. He was crucified for the love of mankind. Consider the infinite degree of that love. Without love for humanity John the Baptist would not have offered his life. It has been likewise with all the Prophets and Holy Souls. If the Báb had not manifested love for mankind, surely He would not have offered His breast for a thousand bullets. If Bahá'u'lláh had not been aflame with love for humanity, He would not have willingly accepted forty years' imprisonment.

Observe how rarely human souls sacrifice their pleasure or comfort for others, how improbable that a man would offer his eye or suffer himself to be dismembered for the benefit of another. Yet all the divine Manifestations suffered, offered Their lives and blood, sacrificed Their existence, comfort and all They possessed for the sake of mankind. . . Were it not for Their love for humanity, spiritual love would be mere nomenclature. Were it not for Their illumination, human souls would not be radiant. How effective is Their love! This is a sign of the love of God, a ray of the Sun of Reality.[52]

'Abdu'l-Bahá

PART II

TO LIVE IN LOVE

Ye have been forbidden in the Book of God to engage in contention and conflict, to strike another, or to commit similar acts whereby hearts and souls may be saddened . . . Wish not for others what ye wish not for yourselves; fear God, and be not of the prideful. Ye are all created out of water, and unto dust shall ye return. Reflect upon the end that awaiteth you, and walk not in the ways of the oppressor. Give ear unto the verses of God which He Who is the sacred Lote-Tree reciteth unto you. They are assuredly the infallible balance, established by God, the Lord of this world and the next.[53]

Bahá'u'lláh

In this sacred Dispensation, conflict and contention are in no wise permitted. Every aggressor deprives himself of God's grace. It is incumbent upon everyone to show the utmost love, rectitude of conduct, straightforwardness and sincere kindliness unto all the peoples and kindreds of the world, be they friends or strangers. So intense must be the spirit of love and loving kindness, that the stranger may find himself a friend, the enemy a true brother, no difference whatsoever existing between them. For universality is of God and all limitations earthly.[54]

'Abdu'l-Bahá

Nothing whatever can, in this Day, inflict a greater harm upon this Cause than dissension and strife, contention, estrangement and apathy, among the loved ones of God.[55]

Bahá'u'lláh

The injunctions in the Bahá'í writings to avoid conflict and all forms of violence are clear and unambiguous. The Bahá'í Faith has come to create peace on our planet, and reveals the necessary means to accomplish this. Some of these concern the organization of all the peoples of the world by means of supranational institutions. Others concern the conditions for creating love within each individual and improving the relationships between individuals. The one is just as necessary as the other, since society affects the attitude and conduct of individuals, and the attitudes of individuals influence the values of society. This presentation will only focus on the change of attitudes which every individual person can make in his or her own life in order that divine love be experienced and translated into action.

The love in the universe is one, but manifests itself, as we have seen, in different ways, thus creating a sort of power circle: love flowing from God to man, from man to man and from man back to God. Man steps into this circle whenever he declares his love for God, through one of His Manifestations. God responds to this love by imparting His love. The individual is then able to share this love with others. The following chapters of this book are ordered accordingly:

- Man's love for God
- To receive God's love
- Love of one's neighbour
- To give lasting happiness to others

MAN'S LOVE FOR GOD 5

Real love is impossible unless one turn his face towards God and be attracted to His Beauty.[56]

'Abdu'l-Bahá

God's love is an eternal power in the universe: it includes all people, whether believers or not. Everyone is potentially able to express this love. When a person declares his faith in God, he is enabled to acquire a conscious relation to God's love, and experience it as a living force in his own life – a force that gives him the strength to be a better human being. It is only when an individual declares his love for God that God's eternal love can fully reach him.

O Son of Being! Love Me, that I may love thee. If thou lovest Me not, My love can in no wise reach thee. Know this, O servant.[57]

Bahá'u'lláh

The essential part of God's revelation consists of guidelines and advice on how an individual can cultivate a loving relationship to an invisible God. Bahá'u'lláh has revealed innumerable prayers and meditations that we may use to express our love to God. Yet it is not only through praisegiving and thankfulness that we should express this love; it should also be expressed through action. To abide by the laws and ordinances included in the revelation is one way of expressing our love, since in doing so we are carrying out the will of our Beloved. In His Book of Laws, the Kitáb-i-Aqdas, Bahá'u'lláh states:

O ye peoples of the world! Know assuredly that My commandments are the lamps of My loving providence among My servants, and the keys of My mercy for My creatures . . .

. . . From My laws the sweet-smelling savour of My garment can be smelled . . . The Tongue of My power hath, from the heaven of My omnipotent glory, addressed to My creation these words: "Observe My commandments, for the love of My beauty." Happy is the lover that hath inhaled the divine fragrance of his Best-Beloved from these words, laden with the perfume of a grace which no tongue can describe.[58]

Bahá'u'lláh

The Holy Writings of the Bahá'í Faith are a God-given assistance to us, both when it comes to expressing our love for God, and with regard to receiving it ourselves and passing it on to others. Among the fundamental prerequisites of maintaining contact with the source of divine love is that every day – morning and evening – we read the Holy Writings. The reading should take place with reverence, attention and thought. The amount read is unimportant; what is important is that we find the spiritual joy and love hidden behind the words, and let this inspire us. We can then lift our spirits to the dawning-place of God's Word and come into contact with the living spiritual power from which it originates.

Another prerequisite for spiritual growth is that each day we recite an obligatory prayer, facing the Shrine of Bahá'u'lláh at Bahjí in the Holy Land. This is also done in a state of joy and love, by opening our inner self to the warming beams of light that flow from the focal point of love, in the same way as flowers open their petals to the sun.

When prayer and calling upon God's spirit is followed by meditation, the spiritual power gathered around us will have the opportunity to influence our soul. We will gain insight and understanding in different matters, finding answers to questions to which we earlier did not manage to find solutions. We will find sadness and afflictions disappear in immense delight. These are bounties which the Holy Spirit imparts to an individual whose heart is open and receptive.

Love must then be converted into action. We can do this by complying with the ideals formulated in the Holy Writings.

Loving-kindness towards all living things is one of the central doctrines in the Writings. Through daily endeavour we will little by little change our attitudes and behaviour towards others.

To share with our fellow beings the gifts God has given us when our lives are filled with joy through faith in God's Manifestation is itself one of the greatest deeds of love we can do.

Unselfish service is the way we express our love in daily life, both through the way we work for the Bahá'í Faith and through the way we carry out our professions – and preeminently, in the way we relate to our fellow men.

How to cultivate the love of God is a topic treated in more detail in my book *Unlocking the Gate of the Heart*.[59] Hence, this book does not cover all the issues presented there. The next section concentrates on one important achievement: namely, submission to God in prayer and meditation, and the forgetting of everything but Him.

To forget everything but God

> The essence of love is for man to turn his heart to the Beloved One, and sever himself from all else but Him, and desire naught save that which is the desire of his Lord.[60]
>
> *Bahá'u'lláh*

So simply does Bahá'u'lláh formulate the essence of love in this passage:
- to turn to God
- to sever ourselves from everything except Him
- to attune our will to God's will

Turning to God is done most directly through prayer and meditation. By reading Bahá'u'lláh's prayers and calling on God with sincerity and devotion, the presence of the Holy Spirit will become a reality. Having called upon it, we can remain in silence and allow all our thoughts, all pictures and associations, to come to rest, and let the spiritual power work within our spirit. In such a state we may experience that what was felt to be a heavy burden can become light and easy. The joy of life may be renewed.

41

Previous annoyances may disappear. We may experience that our mistakes are forgiven; and we find that we are capable as well of forgiving others the wrongs they have done us. The ability to forgive is closely related to the ability to let go of hard feelings towards others. To forget ourselves completely in the presence of God and just be absorbed in His spirit will strengthen our ability to forgive, and thereby our ability to view others in the light of real love and unity.

O Son of Light! Forget all save Me and commune with My spirit. This is of the essence of My command, therefore turn unto it.[61]

Bahá'u'lláh

"Remembrance of God" is an important way of achieving the ability to free oneself from this world and attach oneself to God. To remember God can be done simply by calling upon God. Or a longer meditation recommended in the Holy Writings can be performed, consisting in the repetition of the Greatest Name, "Alláh-u-Abhá", a certain number of times each day (See Part III, Spiritual exercise no. 1). This repetition makes us forget everything else, as we just "remember", i.e. give all our attention to God. The reading of the Writings every morning and evening and the performance of the obligatory prayers help us to remember God as well. During the day we will normally have plenty of opportunities to call upon God and quickly direct our thoughts towards His spirit.

Whoso reciteth, in the privacy of his chamber, the verses revealed by God, the scattering angels of the Almighty shall scatter abroad the fragrance of the words uttered by his mouth, and shall cause the heart of every righteous man to throb. Though he may, at first, remain unaware of its effect, yet the virtue of the grace vouchsafed unto him must needs sooner or later exercise its influence upon his soul. Thus have the mysteries of the Revelation of God been decreed by virtue of the Will of Him Who is the Source of power and wisdom.[62]

Bahá'u'lláh

To dedicate oneself to God, to place one's trust in His omnipotence and love, is the only thing that can give a person lasting peace and joy of heart. God *is* love and joy, and God is eternal. All the small and often egotistical pleasures we are able to obtain for ourselves last only for a short while.

O Son of Spirit! There is no peace for thee save by renouncing thyself and turning unto Me; for it behoveth thee to glory in My name, not in thine own; to put thy trust in Me and not in thyself, since I desire to be loved alone and above all that is.[63]

Bahá'u'lláh

O Son of Man! Wert thou to speed through the immensity of space and traverse the expanse of heaven, yet thou wouldst find no rest save in submission to Our command and humbleness before Our Face.[64]

Bahá'u'lláh

In many prayers Bahá'u'lláh and 'Abdu'l-Bahá refer to the state of being consciously empty-minded, which is necessary if we are to be reunited with God's spirit. It is necessary that we practise entering this state, so as to make ourselves susceptible to the influences of the Holy Spirit.

O God, teach us Thy Oneness and give us a realization of Thy Unity, that we may see no one save Thee. Thou art the Merciful and the Giver of bounty!

O God, create in the hearts of Thy beloved the fire of Thy love, that it may consume the thought of everything save Thee.

Reveal to us, O God, Thine exalted eternity – that Thou hast ever been and wilt ever be, and that there is no God save Thee. Verily, in Thee will we find comfort and strength.[65]

Bahá'u'lláh

O Lord, my God! . . . Help me to be selfless at the heavenly entrance of Thy gate, and aid me to be detached from all things within Thy holy precincts. Lord! Give me to drink from the chalice of selflessness; with its robe clothe me, and in its ocean immerse me. Make me as dust in the pathway of Thy loved ones, and grant that I may offer up my soul for the earth ennobled by the footsteps of Thy chosen ones in Thy path, O Lord of Glory in the Highest.[66]

'Abdu'l-Bahá

TO RECEIVE GOD'S LOVE 6

O Son of Being! With the hands of power I made thee and with the fingers of strength I created thee; and within thee have I placed the essence of My light. Be thou content with it and seek naught else, for My work is perfect and My command is binding. Question it not, nor have a doubt thereof.[67]

Bahá'u'lláh

To forget oneself and to be selfless, in both prayer and action, are important if we are to receive the love of God. However, this is not the same as having a negative view of oneself in relation to other human beings: viewing oneself as essentially sinful, pitiful or unworthy. It is not the same as being helpless or not having enough courage to state one's opinions. It is not the same as acting out of bad conscience, or as viewing oneself as degraded in relation to others. On the contrary: being selfless and humble is, among other things, to be willing to view ourselves in the way God wishes us to, as children He created through love. God is satisfied with His creation, as Bahá'u'lláh makes plain in the words above. He created us with a perfection that we can make the mistake of denying, if we view ourselves as entirely despicable. He created us in His image; but we will never be able to see this image if we are exceedingly concerned with our own imperfections and not open to seeing our innate God-given potential, our higher self. If our way of practising humility and selflessness obstructs the realization of this potential, there is reason to suspect that our concept of humility is false. Perhaps, without realising it, we are making use of this false conception to protect our lower self, our ego, from letting go of something. The only true humility lies in being prepared to fulfil God's will, and to view everyone, including ourselves, as God views us. In the passage above, Bahá'u'lláh warns us against questioning the perfection of God's creation, and by this He means you and me!

One of the greatest of God's gifts to human beings is the promise that we are loved by Him, that His love lives in every one of us and is with us wherever we may roam, that we are given a divine spirit and that we can rejoice in God's love in eternal delight. To open our heart, our emotions and intellect to receive this is one of the most important things we can do to fulfil our own life as God wants us to do, and at the same time to become able to treat others in accordance with God's will.

> O Son of Bounty! Out of the wastes of nothingness, with the clay of My command I made thee to appear, and have ordained for thy training every atom in existence and the essence of all created things. Thus, ere thou didst issue from thy mother's womb, I destined for thee two founts of gleaming milk, eyes to watch over thee, and hearts to love thee. Out of My loving-kindness, 'neath the shade of My mercy I nurtured thee, and guarded thee by the essence of My grace and favour. And My purpose in all this was that thou mightest attain My everlasting dominion and become worthy of My invisible bestowals . . . [68]
>
> *Bahá'u'lláh*

You are given an alternative way of looking at things

> O Man of Two Visions! Close one eye and open the other. Close one to the world and all that is therein, and open the other to the hallowed beauty of the Beloved.[69]
>
> *Bahá'u'lláh*

God has given human beings the capacity to see and experience the world in different ways. To change our experience of the world means to enter a new world. Of course, the world around us has not changed objectively, although at times it may seem so, but certainly our own emotional reactions to the world will alter, and with our reactions the way we conduct ourselves. Spiritual development means therefore, among other things, to develop other ways of experiencing ourselves and the world, so as to change our feelings and succeed in acting differently. Spiritual development is impossible without being open to such a perspective.

As we grow up, we learn to adapt to the demands of the material world in order to survive. The processes of learning how to control our own body, learning language and social skills, are of course necessary. But the motivation to survive physically may cover up another conception of ourselves and the world, a spiritual conception. Fortunately we are all born holy, with a pure heart; and Bahá'u'lláh counsels us that as adults we should find our way back to that spiritual purity, if we have lost it after having mastered these material skills.

> . . . every individual is born holy and pure, and only thereafter may he become defiled.[70]
>
> *'Abdu'l-Bahá*

> The hearts of all children are of the utmost purity. They are mirrors upon which no dust has fallen.[71]
>
> *'Abdu'l-Bahá*

> O Son of Spirit! My first counsel is this: Possess a pure, kindly and radiant heart, that thine may be a sovereignty ancient, imperishable and everlasting.[72]
>
> *Bahá'u'lláh*

When searching for the pure heart, we must be willing to set aside what we have learnt from studies and reading, and to leave behind our bitter experiences, as well as our frantic obsessions with pleasure and entertainment. Eventually, we will uncover our true heart again, our true individuality, our innermost, deepest voice.

> O Son of Being! Thy heart is My home; sanctify it for My descent. Thy spirit is My place of revelation; cleanse it for My manifestation.[73]
>
> *Bahá'u'lláh*

To achieve this, we will make use of all the strength and ability we have developed throughout life, in order to reestablish contact with the pure heart without becoming naive or childish. Yet, even if we use all we have learnt, it is evident that the solution does not lie within the limitations which all these abilities and experiences have given us. It is this realization that Bahá'u'lláh probably refers to when in the following passage He admonishes us to make our eyes blind, to close our ears, to free ourselves from all knowledge and to detach ourselves from earthly riches. To close the physical senses literally is, of course, not what this is about; we must learn to close the window in ourselves that opens on love of the material world, so as to open some new senses. For God has bestowed upon us opportunities and insights which completely surpass all material and intellectual limitations: we are given another eye, an eye of the heart that can see God's beauty; we are given a spiritual ear that we can use for listening to the depths of His words; we are given knowledge that is not conditioned by learning.

> O Son of Dust! Blind thine eyes, that thou mayest behold My beauty; stop thine ears, that thou mayest hearken unto the sweet melody of My voice; empty thyself of all learning, that thou mayest partake of My knowledge; and sanctify thyself from riches, that thou mayest obtain a lasting share from the ocean of My eternal wealth. Blind thine eyes, that is, to all save My beauty; stop thine ears to all save My word; empty thyself of all learning save the knowledge of Me; that with a clear vision, a pure heart and an attentive ear thou mayest enter the court of My holiness.[74]
> *Bahá'u'lláh*

God's creation of the world means that all that He created – minerals, plants, animals and human beings – was to be a reflection of His qualities. Therefore the world is like a book which, if we read it in the correct way, can teach us something about God. God deposited all His names and qualities as a potential in the human soul. Spiritual development means letting this spiritual potential be activated and made real through human life. If we turn our gaze inwards, we will find the essence of the entire material universe enfolded within us. These are the archetypal powers that Bahá'u'lláh, through His life and revelation, wanted to exploit and bring into operation, and which are among the great gifts of divine love.

You are forgiven your mistakes

The insight that humanity is one and that to God all people are equal is in reality a great gift for all of us, and especially to you, who might be inclined to think that you are a little less worthy than others. If you look closely at the principle of the unity of mankind, and think about it, you will understand that the idea that you are intrinsically "worse" than others is your own notion, not God's opinion about you. Perhaps other people have told you that you are bad, not worth loving when you do "so and so". Now you can safely put away these thoughts. You have declared your love to God, and that is the only condition needed for Him to return His love to you. Of course, no person is perfect in any regard, and you may find that even you have a few imperfections, aspects you want to improve. You can always accomplish this later. The most important thing is that you feel you are good enough for God right now.

Original sin is not a concept in the Bahá'í Faith. You need not worry about being the heir to a sin committed by Adam and Eve in the early morning of time. Sin is a concept used about actions which are not in accordance with God's will. Bahá'u'lláh promises the forgiveness of sins to those who recognize and admit their faults to God, and who are willing to correct their behaviour. Even to the worst criminal He promises this, so why not to you and me?

> Thou art that All-Bountiful Who art not deterred by a multitude of sins from vouchsafing Thy bounty, and the flow of Whose gifts is not arrested by the withdrawal of the peoples of the world. From eternity the door of Thy grace hath remained wide open. A dewdrop out of the ocean of Thy mercy is able to adorn all things with the ornament of sanctity, and a sprinkling of the waters of Thy bounty can cause the entire creation to attain unto true wealth.

. . . Thy mercy hath embraced the whole creation, and Thy grace hath pervaded all things. From the billows of the ocean of Thy generosity the seas of eagerness and enthusiasm were revealed.[75]

Bahá'u'lláh

To ask God for forgiveness is something you can do whenever you feel free to. No other person can forgive you on God's behalf. Your sins are a matter between you and God.

I am a sinner, O my Lord, and Thou art the Ever-Forgiving. As soon as I recognized Thee, I hastened to attain the exalted court of Thy loving-kindness. Forgive me, O my Lord, my sins which have hindered me from walking in the ways of Thy good pleasure, and from attaining the shores of the ocean of Thy oneness.

There is no one, O my Lord, who can deal bountifully with me to whom I can turn my face, and none who can have compassion on me that I may crave his mercy. Cast me not out, I implore Thee, of the presence of Thy grace, neither do Thou withhold from me the outpourings of Thy generosity and bounty. Ordain for me, O my Lord, what Thou hast ordained for them that love Thee, and write down for me what Thou hast written down for Thy chosen ones. My gaze hath, at all times, been fixed on the horizon of Thy gracious providence, and mine eyes bent upon the court of Thy tender mercies. Do with me as beseemeth Thee. No God is there but Thee, the God of power, the God of glory, Whose help is implored by all men.[76]

Bahá'u'lláh

You are an eternal being

Is life finished when we die? If the answer is yes, you will be in a hurry to collect all the pleasures life may offer you. Other people will only become interesting to you when they help you make life more pleasant. It will be a matter of throwing yourself into everyone's fight against everyone else in order to secure the tidbits for yourself. Any obstacle in reaching this goal will irritate you, will eventually make you aggressive, or may be experienced as threatening and fill you with anxiety. To lose something you feel you strongly need can be experienced as a catastrophe, and the ensuing desperation will drive you wild, even violent, in your pursuit of pleasure, if you do not simply give up and end your life in bottomless despair.

If our lower self is permitted to get its way, this will be more or less how we experience the world. In this world view, divine love is badly off. Inner peace does not exist. All happiness is of short duration and needs to be defended, so that we do not lose it so soon as to cause despair and depression – and attack may turn out to be the best defence.

Among the greatest gifts of love that God gives us is the assurance that the world is not as our ego – our lower, animal self – spontaneously sees it. God assures us that we are something much, much more than the small, frightened animal that has to fight its way through a threatening world where the laws of the jungle rule. Seen through God's eyes, you and I are eternal beings. We each have a soul that will last through all of God's worlds. We are not essentially our physical bodies – these will die when they no longer serve a purpose – we are essentially eternal souls. The greatest pleasures life can offer are absolutely not conditioned by the body; they rather depend on the condition of the soul.

Aggression is the most common response when something is experienced as threatening. Yet what is capable of threatening something that is eternal? Perishability cannot take anything away from it, since loss is non-existent in the eternal world. What can threaten you when you have nothing to lose? Why be aggressive and enraged when you are not threatened, when you do not have anything that needs to be defended because it cannot be attacked, when you know you do not have to fight for your joys, but are given them freely by God's spirit?

O Son of Man! Thou art My dominion and My dominion perisheth not; wherefore fearest thou thy perishing? Thou art My light and My light shall never be extinguished; why dost thou dread extinction? Thou art My glory and My glory fadeth not;

thou art My robe and My robe shall never be outworn. Abide then in thy love for Me, that thou mayest find Me in the realm of glory.[77]

Bahá'u'lláh

Your true strength is God's love

For every one of you his paramount duty is to choose for himself that on which no other may infringe and none usurp from him. Such a thing – and to this the Almighty is My witness – is the love of God, could ye but perceive it.

Build ye for yourselves such houses as the rain and floods can never destroy, which shall protect you from the changes and chances of this life. This is the instruction of Him Whom the world hath wronged and forsaken.[78]

Bahá'u'lláh

Sometimes our modesty hinders us from choosing the best. We may believe we are not worthy of the best, yet as we go to the back of the line we regard ourselves as a pretty good person! But this principle does not count when you are dealing with God's love, for that is infinite, and no matter how much you receive of it, it will not be to the loss of others. There is still an infinite amount of love for an infinite number of people. Actually, the more you receive of it yourself, the more others receive as well! Perhaps this is why Bahá'u'lláh says it is our duty to choose God's love.

God's love, being of God, is eternal. At the same time, it lives inside us, in you and me. For God can reveal Himself in every heart:

. . . the heart is the throne, in which the Revelation of God the All-Merciful is centred . . .[79]

Bahá'u'lláh

It is almost incomprehensible that every one of us (including me, of all people!) is given such an incredible gift, a gift of kindness and happiness that cannot be lost. Everything else perishes, yet

God's love lasts for ever. If we step into this love which God has given us as a gift that we are entitled to keep in our heart, then all hostility will disappear, fears and anxiety will vanish, and we will gain security and trust. We can go everywhere with confidence. We need this security if we are to be capable of giving love to others, if we are to be capable of serving God and our fellow men in freedom and joy, if we are to be able to give without being afraid to lose.

> O Son of Being! My love is My stronghold; he that entereth therein is safe and secure, and he that turneth away shall surely stray and perish.[80]
>
> *Bahá'u'lláh*

> O Son of Utterance! Thou art My stronghold; enter therein that thou mayest abide in safety. My love is in thee, know it, that thou mayest find Me near unto thee.[81]
>
> *Bahá'u'lláh*

You are noble

> O Son of Spirit! I created thee rich, why dost thou bring thyself down to poverty? Noble I made thee, wherewith dost thou abase thyself? Out of the essence of knowledge I gave thee being, why seekest thou enlightenment from anyone beside Me? Out of the clay of love I moulded thee, how dost thou busy thyself with another? Turn thy sight unto thyself, that thou mayest find Me standing within thee, mighty, powerful and self-subsisting.[82]
>
> *Bahá'u'lláh*

Bahá'u'lláh tells us in this passage that we are created rich, noble, loving and knowledgeable. All people are created in this way, no matter how much they own in the material world, regardless of what status they have in society, regardless of whether they know how to read or write, of whether their IQ is high or low, or whether they are regarded as brutal or sensitive. The secret lies within the last sentence: God has revealed Himself in my own heart; there He is, regardless of the experiences I have had in this world, regardless of all the characteristics others have given me, unaffected by my self-critique or my feeling of being unsuccessful, inferior or impotent. Do we dare to open ourselves to believe what Bahá'u'lláh is telling us? Do we dare to base ourselves on the fact that we have an inherent dignity because of God's presence in our hearts, that we have what we need if only we can come into the powerful presence of God, that we have all the knowledge we need if only we communicate with Him in our hearts, that we have all the love we need if we dare to let God's voice in?

Such a declaration of trust in God's presence in our hearts is also a declaration of trust in ourselves. It states that we put God's loving evaluation of who we are above other people's judgement of us, even above our own judgement of ourselves! If we can manage this, we will find – paradoxically – that our individuality increases at the same time as we identify ourselves more closely with the universal, and in this way come closer to other people.

O Son of him that stood by his own Entity in the Kingdom of his self! Know thou, that I have wafted unto thee all the fragrances of holiness, have fully revealed to thee My word, have perfected through thee My bounty and have desired for thee that which I have desired for My Self. Be then content with My pleasure and thankful unto Me.[83]

Bahá'u'lláh

God's love is eternal happiness

Happiness consists of two kinds: physical and spiritual. The physical happiness is limited; its utmost duration is one day, one month, one year. It hath no result. Spiritual happiness is eternal and unfathomable. This kind of happiness appeareth in one's soul with the love of God and suffereth one to attain to the virtues and perfections of the world of humanity. Therefore, endeavour as much as thou art able in order to illumine the lamp of thy heart by the light of love.[84]

'Abdu'l-Bahá

Happiness and love are inseparable. The world was created out of love, and love is happiness: happiness is the deepest feeling in the universe. The body's feelings will always vary, for the body is subject to the fleeting conditions of the world, but spiritual happiness is bottomless, infinite. Let the soul immerse itself entirely in this joy, and let the body be a sounding board making hymns of joy ring out in this world! The reason for this happiness is that the soul is reunited with the Beloved:

O Son of Man! Rejoice in the gladness of thine heart, that thou mayest be worthy to meet Me and to mirror forth My beauty.[85]

Bahá'u'lláh

O Son of Spirit! The spirit of holiness beareth unto thee the joyful tidings of reunion; wherefore dost thou grieve? The spirit of power confirmeth thee in His cause; why dost thou veil thyself? The light of His countenance doth lead thee; how canst thou go astray?[86]

Bahá'u'lláh

God's light shines through you

O Son of Being! Thou art My lamp and My light is in thee. Get thou from it thy radiance and seek none other than Me. For I have created thee rich and have bountifully shed My favour upon thee.[87]

Bahá'u'lláh

God's light is shining in us. God's light is love and insight. These treasures lie hidden in our heart. We do not need to look for anyone to give us these things when we already have them in our own inner self. We do not need to engage ourselves in pleasure-hunting. We carry the largest of all joys in our own heart. Every day, every hour of the day, we can search for this light in our inner self, and listen to the thoughts filled with love that our higher self inside us is thinking. These thoughts tell us that we are loved, that we are appreciated, that we carry the holy light within us; they speak to us like this:

O My Friend! Thou art the daystar of the heavens of My holiness, let not the defilement of the world eclipse thy splendour. Rend asunder the veil of heedlessness, that from behind the clouds thou mayest emerge resplendent and array all things with the apparel of life.[88]

Bahá'u'lláh

The light we carry inside us is not to be hidden, it must shine upon the world. The rays must stand forth and let others take part in the happiness that is given us. To hide our light under a bushel is to let our ego hinder the light from shining for others. Many of us have learnt that we should be careful of showing our strength. We are afraid of seeming superior or patronising; afraid of seeming arrogant or insolent. True, the ego's self-assertion may go beyond all limits, and we can abuse our own strength in order to rise above others, to view ourselves as better, as innocent or unique. The result is arrogance. The darkness of the ego cannot create light.

But what Bahá'u'lláh encourages us to do is to stand forth with the light *He* gives us. He asks us to be lanterns for *His* light, channels for *His* love. It is not with ourselves that we stand forth, but with the spirit of unity, a spirit that is universal and accessible to all people. He asks us to step back with our own feelings and favourite ideas, and make ourselves the tool for this power. When love is the driving force, love is the result. Light will create light, and when faced with light, darkness has no existence.

Bahá'u'lláh gives us the task of bringing the light of unity to the world. He asks us not to overlook the talents and powers He has given us. He asks us to take the gifts He has brought us, and pass them on to others. He promises to assist everyone who assists Him. We are never alone, for He is invisibly by our side.

O friends! Be not careless of the virtues with which ye have been endowed, neither be neglectful of your high destiny . . . Ye are the stars of the heaven of understanding, the breeze that stirreth at the break of day, the soft-flowing waters upon which must depend the very life of all men, the letters inscribed upon His sacred scroll.[89]

Bahá'u'lláh

We can quickly feel unworthy when we see that we are the ones Bahá'u'lláh is referring to here. We may be afraid that someone will expect more of us than we can offer; we may feel that we are not worthy in this context. We may be afraid our ego will have megalomaniac dreams, become self-satisfied and swaggering. It may be a wise idea to ask yourself what voice inside you is telling you this. You must not let your ego trick you into hiding the light given to you. You must also not allow your ego to abuse the Word of God in order to increase its own conceitedness. You are the only person who can give the correct answer to this question. Listen to what your higher self thinks of this, because God assures us that the truth lies within us.

It is certain that you will never manage to fulfil these exhortations of Bahá'u'lláh if you act motivated by a heavy feeling of guilt, or by fear of not being good enough. Only when your actions derive from a securely founded inner freedom and happiness, when you act without feeling pressured either by the expectations of others or your own obsessions – only then will you be able to be a channel for the "breezes of spring" that God wishes to send to the world through you:

O people of Bahá! Ye are the breezes of spring that are wafted over the world. Through you We have adorned the world of being with the ornament of the knowledge of the Most Merciful. Through you the countenance of the world hath been wreathed in smiles, and the brightness of His light shone forth. Cling ye to the Cord of steadfastness, in such wise that all vain imaginings may utterly vanish. Speed ye forth from the horizon of power, in the name of your Lord, the Unconstrained, and announce unto His servants, with wisdom and eloquence, the tidings of this Cause, whose splendour hath been shed upon the world of being. Beware lest anything withhold you from observing the things prescribed unto you by the Pen of Glory, as it moved over His Tablet with sovereign majesty and might. Great is the blessedness of him that hath hearkened to its shrill voice, as it was raised, through the power of truth, before all who are in heaven and all who are on earth . . . O people of Bahá! The river that is Life indeed hath flowed for your sakes. Quaff ye in My name, despite them that have disbelieved in God, the Lord of Revelation. We have made you to be the hands of Our Cause. Render ye victorious this Wronged One, Who hath been sore-tried in the hands of the workers of iniquity. He, verily, will aid every one that aideth Him, and will remember every one that remembereth Him. To this beareth witness this Tablet that hath shed the splendour of the loving-kindness of your Lord, the All-Glorious, the All-Compelling.[90]

Bahá'u'lláh

Difficulties are God's love in disguise

O Son of Man! My calamity is My providence, outwardly it is fire and vengeance, but inwardly it is light and mercy. Hasten thereunto that thou mayest become an eternal light and an immortal spirit. This is My command unto thee, do thou observe it.[91]

Bahá'u'lláh

Accidents, difficulties and painful experiences are not meaningless. Bahá'u'lláh encourages us to meet the pain actively and not to turn aside or hide. The flame of love can also burn when what we need is "strong measures" to let go of our love of the world. Many people experience that it is when despair is at its worst that God's help is closest.

O Son of Man! For everything there is a sign. The sign of love is fortitude under My decree and patience under My trials.[92]

Bahá'u'lláh

O Son of Man! If adversity befall thee not in My path, how canst thou walk in the ways of them that are content with My pleasure? If trials afflict thee not in thy longing to meet Me, how wilt thou attain the light in thy love for My beauty?[93]

Bahá'u'lláh

We have to trust that God's spirit will always be there so that we can make the best of every situation. The power of God's love is so strong that we need not be afraid:

The power of Thy might beareth me witness, O my Well-Beloved! Every limb of my body, methinks, is endowed with a tongue that glorifieth Thee and magnifieth Thy name. Armed with the power of Thy love, the hatred which moveth them that are against Thee can never alarm me; and with Thy praise on my lips, the rulings of Thy decree can in no wise fill me with sorrow. Fortify, therefore, Thy love within my breast, and suffer me to face the assaults which all the peoples of the earth may launch against me. I swear by Thee! Every hair of my head proclaimeth: "But for the adversities that befall me in Thy path, how could I ever taste the divine sweetness of Thy tenderness and love?"[94]

Bahá'u'lláh

It may help us to view our difficulties as sent from God in order to make us learn. By asking our higher self what we are to learn in a given situation, resources and insight that we barely dreamed of will appear from within. It is in the critical situations, when we are bewildered, confused or resigned, when nothing we try for ourselves seems to work – it is in just these situations that we are given susceptibility and openness to listen to what the Holy Spirit whispers to us. Having a dialogue with one's higher self is actually possible. And it turns out that something inside us knows things we had no idea we knew!

It is manifest that beyond this material body, man is endowed with another reality, which is the world of exemplars constituting the heavenly body of man. In speaking, man says, "I saw", "I spoke", "I went". Who is this *I*? It is obvious that this *I* is different from this body. It is clear that when man is thinking, it is as though he were consulting with some other person. With whom is he consulting? It is evident that it is another reality, or one aside from this body, with whom he enters into consultations when he thinks, "Shall I do this work or not?" "What will be the result of my doing this?" Or when he questions the other reality, "What is the objection to this work if I do it?" And then that reality in man communicates its opinion to him concerning the point at issue. Therefore, that reality in man is clearly and obviously other than his body – an ego with which man enters into consultation and whose opinion man seeks . . .

Furthermore, man sees in the world of dreams. He travels in the East; he travels in the West; although his body is stationary, his body is here. It is that reality in him which makes the journey while the body sleeps. There is no doubt that a reality exists other than the outward, physical reality . . .

This other and inner reality is called the heavenly body, the ethereal form which corresponds to this body. This is the conscious reality which discovers the inner meaning of things, for the outer body of man does not discover anything. The inner ethereal reality grasps the mysteries of existence, discovers scientific truths and indicates their technical application . . .

. . . this human reality stands between the higher and the lower in man, between the world of the animal and the world of Divinity. When the animal proclivity in man becomes predominant, he sinks even lower than the brute. When the heavenly powers are triumphant in his nature, he becomes the noblest and most superior being in the world of creation . . .

The holy Manifestations of God come into the world to dispel the darkness of the animal, or physical, nature of man, to purify him from his imperfections in order that his heavenly and spiritual nature may become quickened, his divine qualities awakened, his perfections visible, his potential powers revealed and all the virtues of the world of humanity latent within him may come to life . . .

Were it not for the coming of these holy Manifestations of God, all mankind would be found on the plane of the animal.[95]

'Abdu'l-Bahá

Those who have become intoxicated by the love of God, and have mastered their own ego, have nothing to fear when it comes to difficulties:

As for you, O ye lovers of God, make firm your steps in His Cause, with such resolve that ye shall not be shaken though the direst of calamities assail the world. By nothing, under no conditions, be ye perturbed. Be ye anchored fast as the high mountains, be stars that dawn over the horizon of life, be bright lamps in the gatherings of unity, be souls humble and lowly in the presence of the friends, be innocent in heart. Be ye symbols of guidance and lights of godliness, severed from the world, clinging to the handhold that is sure and strong, spreading abroad the spirit of life, riding the Ark of salvation . . .

By the life of Bahá! Only he who is severed from the world shall achieve this ultimate grace, he who is a captive of divine love, empty of passion and self, from every aspect true unto his God, humble, lowly, supplicating, in tears, submissive in the presence of the Lord.[96]

'Abdu'l-Bahá

God is always with you

You are never alone. God's eye sees everything; the presence of God, which is in everything, looks upon you with love and care. God remembers you. Therefore He asks us to remember Him. In this way we achieve contact both ways; in this way we can take part in the inexplicable joy that always accompanies divine love:

We remember every one of you, men and women, and from this Spot – the Scene of incomparable glory – regard you all as one soul and send you the joyous tidings of divine blessings which have preceded all created things, and of My remembrance that pervadeth everyone, whether young or old. The glory of God rest upon you, O people of Bahá. Rejoice with exceeding gladness through My remembrance, for He is indeed with you at all times.[97]

Bahá'u'lláh

The Abhá Beauty endured the most afflictive of calamities. He bore countless agonies and ills. He enjoyed not a moment's peace, drew not an easeful breath. He wandered, homeless, over desert sands and mountain slopes; He was shut in a fortress, and a prison cell. But to Him, His pauper's mat of straw was an eternal throne of glory, and His heavy chains a sovereign's carcanet. By day, by night, He lived under a whirring sword, and He was ready from moment to moment for death on the cross. He bore all this that He might purify the world, and deck it out with the tender mercies of the Lord God; that He might set it at rest; that conflict and aggression might be put to flight, the lance and the keen blade be exchanged for loving fellowship, malevolence and war turn into safety and gentleness and love, that battlefields of hate and wrath should become gardens of delight, and places where once the blood-drenched armies clashed, be fragrant pleasure grounds; that warfare should be seen as shame, and the resort to arms, even as a loathsome sickness, be shunned by every people; that universal peace raise its pavilions on the loftiest mounts, and war be made to perish forever from the earth.

Wherefore must the loved ones of God, laboriously, with the waters of their striving, tend and nourish and foster this tree of hope. In whatsoever land they dwell, let them with a whole heart befriend and be companions to those who are either close to them, or far removed. Let them, with qualities like unto those of heaven, promote the institutions and the religion of God. Let them never lose heart, never be despondent, never feel afflicted. The more antagonism they meet, the more let them show their own good faith; the more torments and calamities they have to face, the more generously let them pass round the bounteous cup. Such is the spirit which will become the life of the world, such is the spreading light at its heart: and he who may be and do other than this is not worthy to serve at the Holy Threshold of the Lord.[98]

'Abdu'l-Bahá

Bahá'u'lláh and 'Abdu'l-Bahá showed us through their lives what true love for one's neighbour is. In their writings they highlight this theme, teaching us how to go about things so that altruistic love becomes a motivating force in our own lives. Many of us, however, may feel that the ideals shown by these towering figures are so high that it would be impossible to live up to their example without overstraining ourselves. It is tempting to believe that it will only be possible to fulfil these ideals in a future society.

But perhaps it is possible to view things in another way. First of all, we will never reach an ideal future society, if true love does not animate the people who are to build that society. This makes the living of true love here and now a challenge for every one of us. True love is not something we can expect as the outcome of a special arrangement of society; true love has to do with choices made by individual human beings. It is a power permeating everything, and it is always here and now. Our contribution to a better society in future is to practise it daily.

Fear of striving after high ideals often stems from the notion that we will stretch ourselves too far, leave our real identity behind, and become alienated from the person we actually wish to be. Notions like these may be founded on a belief that guilt feelings and a joyless sense of duty are necessary to realize true love. But can we actually believe that what the writings ask us to do is to flog ourselves so as to become kind and noble? Would this be to behave in a loving way? The answer is pretty obvious: to force oneself to be kind, or for that matter to force others to be kind, cannot be true love. However, the fear of punishment and the hope of reward – which are also important in the Bahá'í teachings – may be attitudes that once formed our own charac-ters and our own patterns of reaction throughout our childhood, when various figures of authority wished to shape us to conform to what they considered to be a well-behaved child. The fear of not being accepted and loved could be a strong discipline; shame and guilt may then have been what we experienced or feared we would experience in punishment.

The basis for practising true love towards others is the belief that God has true love for all human beings. You and I are no exceptions; and to claim that one is a special case in this cosmic law can only be an expression of the ego and not of divine understanding. If I believe that God cares about me, it cannot possibly be right that I have to flog myself at the same time, and force myself to relate to matters in ways that I presently am unable to do or do not want to do. Inner freedom and happiness are dimensions of true love that God does not wish us to take away from ourselves, through insane efforts at reaching an ideal.

The first step towards becoming truly loving people is therefore to let go of the idea that God demands sacrifices from us that we do not wish to offer. Love does not demand that kind of sacrifice. But he who has love is willing to make sacrifices, since it will happen in freedom and joy. Love has then become the motive for carrying out the sacrifice. And this is the point we have to reach: where love has become our driving force. To get there, we must, strangely enough, stop regarding love as some distant ideal we have to strive to reach some day in the future. We must trust that love is simply here and now. We must trust that this love is capable of accepting me, with all my mistakes and imperfections, just here and now.

Such an idea involves a thorough inner reorientation for many of us who have been raised to be kind and compliant, and have brought these attitudes with us into the Bahá'í community. For us it is necessary to stop stretching ourselves to do things others want us to do, just because we feel it is expected of us. If I give a gift or if I make a sacrifice, it must be because I want to do so myself. It is possible to sincerely wish to do what others want from me – in freedom. If I voluntarily give my gift, and even give it as a gift to the eternal God, it strengthens my own freedom, it does not degrade me at all. Such a gift, given in inner freedom, does not give the receiver any expectations of returned favours. If the receiver feels that he incurs a debt of gratitude when he receives a gift, he will be in danger of losing his own inner freedom and will perhaps act out of what he thinks the other person expects him to do. But all people are set free to act out of their own accord, and for God's sake alone. Whether we bind or set free those who receive our gifts and sacrifices depends on our own inner freedom, our own love. Those gifts that are given with love are given in freedom and joy, and will set others free as well.

This is also obviously important to consider if you are in the position of the receiver. If we always believe there are obligations connected with receiving a gift, we will risk turning down gifts that are given with a pure heart, and in this way hinder God's love from reaching us.

We should not let high ideals and ideal solutions enslave us and cause a loss of inner freedom, just as we do not let other people's expectations rule our actions. It is clear that motivations that are based on guilty feelings, fear of not being good enough, or ambitions to show off are all given to us by our lower self, our ego. It is only our higher self that can give us the motivation to live divine love, which is a part of that higher self. This means that if we are to take hold of this higher form of love, it is impossible to use means of reaching it that are unknown to it. We cannot become more loving by forcing love in ourselves. We can only become more loving by accepting ourselves where we are, no matter where this is in relation to our ideals, and then by doing what we can to improve from this starting position. If others are of the opinion that this is not good enough, it does not matter. We know that we actually are loved by God such as He created us, and we are able to choose to make ourselves channels for this power of love so it can reach both ourselves and others. God's love is always perfect because it is God's, not our own. Our defects cannot take anything away from what eternally belongs to God. Hence, we should not be worried that we have some flaws and defects. Ours is to practise not letting our flaws hinder divine love from working through us. Every day when we say the short obligatory prayer, we testify to this perspective: we testify to how powerless we are and to God's strength, thereby accepting all the limitations we have as material bodies, and at the same time declaring that God's strength is present and is working through us. The strength of God is our real strength, while the strength of our ego is our biggest weakness.

Being a channel for the Holy Spirit

Being a tool of divine love is like being a channel. The most important aspect of a channel is that it does not hinder things from flowing through it, nor change their quality. It is not the material the channel is made of that is of interest; on the contrary, it is the hollow space – the empty space in the middle, and the openings that allow things to flow in and out – that are the characteristics of a channel.

Being a channel for divine love implies letting a spiritual power flow through you. Hence, you need an empty space within, and an openness both to receive and to let go. When something leaves, the channel will automatically be filled from the other side, as long as you are connected with the infinite power reserves of divine love. In the very moment you give away divine love, you will receive just as much of it. If you give away knowledge about God, you will receive knowledge about God. To teach is to learn.

What the channel itself is made of is of no interest. An implication of the principle of the Holy Spirit is that we can be channels for a spiritual power that knows more and accomplishes more than we can by ourselves. Every one of us, without exception, has limitations, because limitations are characteristic of the material world. The world in which the Holy Spirit operates is, on the contrary, without limit.

> Turn your faces away from the contemplation of your own finite selves and fix your eyes upon the Everlasting Radiance; then will your souls receive in full measure the Divine Power of the Spirit and the Blessings of the Infinite Bounty.
>
> If you thus keep yourselves in readiness, you will become to the world of humanity a burning flame, a star of guidance, and a fruitful tree, changing all its darkness and woe into light and joy by the shining of the Sun of Mercy and the infinite blessings of the Glad Tidings.
>
> This is the meaning of the power of the Holy Spirit, which I pray may be bountifully showered upon you.[99]
>
> *'Abdu'l-Bahá*

To practise the principle of the Holy Spirit in a given situation may mean the following: You are in a situation where you have no idea how to solve a problem. You have reached your own limit, and acknowledged that it has been reached. You can do nothing more without forcing yourself over your own limits, without turning aggressive or stepping on others, without destroying or humiliating yourself in your own eyes. But you have faith in God's love and do not believe that God wants you to apply forceful and violent measures to yourself, as this would mean strengthening your ego. You may, for instance, be involved in a situation with another person in which you do not have the faintest idea what to do. Emotions are running high, and you know you are in danger of doing something that breaks with the ethical principles of the Faith. Or you may be performing an important mission for the Cause and all ways out seem to be closed, so that you are unable to fulfil your objective. In this situation – whatever it is – you restrain yourself, you acknowledge your powerlessness, you turn your inner eye towards God, you call on His spirit and ask for His help. Then you step back, in the belief that something may happen. And something does happen, after a couple of seconds, some minutes, hours or days: a new insight may suddenly take shape, you can hear yourself think in a way you have never experienced before, something happens around you, with the people involved in the situation, something unexplainable can make things fall into the place where they belong, and new possibilities are revealed: the problem is solved in a way you could not foresee. The Holy Spirit has heard your prayer and come to your assistance. It is a living, intelligent and creative force which can be experienced in situations where you yourself have arrived at an impasse.

Often it is in this way: we have to run into a critical situation before we become willing to admit our own powerlessness and summon the assistance of the Holy Spirit. The difficulties, the critical situations, therefore become important catalysts in learning to contact the spiritual power. Active service for the Faith, combined with close and responsible relationships with fellow human beings, will offer many situations where we will have the opportunity to experience this. And you will soon find that those you consider your worst enemies, the most despicable of those surrounding you, may be of great help to you in putting this force to use. Your worst enemy can become your best helper when it comes to spiritual growth. Could there be any better reason for loving your enemies?

Yet it would be sad if we were to experience this wonderful power of love only in uncertain and painful situations. We know and have experienced that when Bahá'ís meet in unity, the atmosphere is filled with joy. We may have experienced the same atmosphere during consultations at the Faith's institutions. We also have the possibility of experiencing the power of the Holy Spirit in other situations, chiefly in meditation and prayer. In a letter to a Bahá'í, 'Abdu'l-Bahá tells in detail about direct experience with the Holy Spirit:

> Know thou, that letter sent to thee by me, was only because of my perfect love for thee and my pity upon thee, for I had the desire that the fragrance of the Holy Spirit, which hath perfumed all regions and imbued the entire body of the world with the Spirit of Life, should pass over thee and abide with thee. Notwithstanding the high position it occupieth, still, with an eloquent tongue, through which the Spirit moveth, hearts are attracted and bosoms burn, it speaketh to the pure hearts and to the good and righteous souls in every spot of the earth. This is the powerful Spirit, the dazzling light, the brilliant star and the overwhelming and universal abundance. And, from its traces, spread and divulged everywhere, thou wilt know and realize its influence and comprehend its radiance. I ask God to expose thee to its fragrance, move thee by its breeze, enkindle thee by its coals of fire and illuminate thee by its brightness. Turn thyself wholly to it – thus thou shalt be enabled to ascertain its influence and power, the strength of its life and the greatness of its confirmation. Verily, I say unto thee, that if for the appearance of that Divine Essence thou desirest to have a definite proof, an indisputable testimony and a strong, convincing evidence, thou must prepare thyself to make thy heart empty and thine eye ready to look only toward the Kingdom of God. Then, at that time, the radiance of that widespread effulgence will descend upon thee successively, and that motion rendered thee by the Holy Spirit will make thee dispense with any other strong evidence that leadeth

to the appearance of this Light, because the greatest and strongest proof for showing the abundance of the Spirit to the bodies is the very appearance of its power and influence to those bodies.[100]

'Abdu'l-Bahá

These statements of 'Abdu'l-Bahá are in many ways astonishingly specific, for they are written with a wish that the recipient of the letter should receive the confirmation of the Holy Spirit. The instructions He gives are for us to use as well. Let us go deeper into it.

"It speaketh to the pure hearts"

'Abdu'l-Bahá first characterizes the Holy Spirit by saying that despite its high position it speaks to the pure hearts and to the good and righteous souls all over the world, in speech ("an eloquent tongue") that attracts the hearts and makes the bosoms glow. This can mean that the Spirit is present wherever there is a pure heart, wherever there is a burning desire to learn God's ways. If anyone should wish to do what God wants, the means with which to do so are there. If you have such a wish and a pure heart, you too will have a voice of truth in your heart, a voice of conscience to guide you.

Of course, it is not easy to know if what you think are thoughts given to you by the Holy Spirit; the majority of our thoughts are not, after all. A pure heart is necessary, that is, a heart which is not dominated by emotions such as desire, anger or disgust. If we pray and meditate daily, and live by the ethical norms given to us by the Faith, and are engaged in service to the Cause, the heart will gradually become pure.

In the process of separating the intuitions given to us by the Holy Spirit from the thoughts of our own ego, the Bahá'í writings will be of great help. The Bahá'í writings are the perfect transcript of the speech of the Holy Spirit to a completely pure and immaculate soul, Bahá'u'lláh. He was authorized by God to establish a new Covenant with people and to stipulate the norms for a new civilization on the planet. We ordinary believers are obviously not given a mandate by the Holy Spirit that in any sort

THE PATH OF LOVE

of way can be compared with God's chosen Manifestation. There is no possibility, therefore, for any conflict between the personal guidance one receives from the Holy Spirit and what is revealed in the Bahá'í writings. If our inner voice should encourage us to break one of the Bahá'í laws, we can be certain that this is not the voice of the Holy Spirit speaking, but our ego, our animal nature, that most likely has taken hold of our imagination. But by connecting our intuitions with the guidance in the writings, and by using the writings as the standard of truth, we will be capable of correcting erroneous apprehensions and little by little draw closer to the correct attitude. It is also important to note that as Bahá'ís we do not have any right to make others follow our inspiration. The insights we have are only valid for ourselves.

The voice of the Holy Spirit within us is the voice of love – through it "hearts are attracted". In all questions that have anything to do with how we should express love towards others, we can utilize this source of inspiration and receive an answer that helps us to behave correctly in the given situation. The Bahá'í writings and the administrative institutions of the Faith together give guidance and direction to people. Of course, they are unable to prescribe the right action for every person in every situation. For this additional guidance, we are given the voice of the Holy Spirit. When we keep to the Covenant, when we abide by the laws Bahá'u'lláh has revealed and are loyal to the administrative institutions He has authorized, we are promised the assistance of the Holy Spirit. Without this assistance we are utterly unable to carry out what the Faith expects us to do, such as teaching the Cause to others. Without this assistance we would not manage to create unity between people.

When it comes to teaching, 'Abdu'l-Bahá promises us in many prayers that we shall be given support from the Holy Spirit that completely surpasses our personal limitations.

O Lord! I am a broken-winged bird and desire to soar in Thy limitless space. How is it possible for me to do this save through Thy providence and grace, Thy confirmation and assistance . . .
O Lord! Should the breath of the Holy Spirit confirm the

weakest of creatures, he would attain all to which he aspireth and would possess anything he desireth . . .[101]

'Abdu'l-Bahá

How to obtain the confirmation of the Holy Spirit

In the last part of the important passage above, 'Abdu'l-Bahá gives specific instructions about how we through meditation can obtain the confirmation of the Holy Spirit, a confirmation that is so convincing that we will stop looking for other proofs. Point by point, 'Abdu'l-Bahá seems to suggest the following:

- You must "make [your] heart empty". This most likely means that you do not engage yourself in thinking your own thoughts, that all mental activity is put to rest, that you find a place in your inner self that is filled with silence and peace.

- You must make your eye "ready to look only toward the Kingdom of God". In the prayer quoted above you have begged God to grant you this confirmation. You keep this sincere wish within you when you proceed into a state of open-minded silence. What will happen next, is only for you to discover.

After you have been united with the Holy Spirit in this state, it may be appropriate to put forward questions you may have, cases where you desire spiritual guidance. The thoughts you then formulate as answers to your own questions will often be inspired by a higher level of insight than you usually have.

This method of seeking the truth must eventually permeate all our services to fellow human beings and to the Cause. The ideas we contribute in consultation within the Faith's administrative institutions may be inspired in this manner as well.

To free the Sun of Truth from the darkness of superstition

It is my hope . . . that these many rivers, each flowing along in diverse and separated beds, will find their way back to the circumambient sea, and merge together and rise up in a single wave of surging oneness; that the unity of truth, through the power of God, will make these illusory differences to vanish away. This is the one essential: for if unity be gained, all other problems will disappear of themselves.[102]

'Abdu'l-Bahá

Humanity is one; truth is also one in reality. Human beings live in a material world and think with their mortal mind, their material consciousness, which emphasizes differences before unity. But to emphasize differences before unity is to let yourself be led by prejudice. To see the limited, not the unlimited power of love that encloses everything, is to close off our access to truth and to give energy to illusions.

Illusions are like dreams; they take the place of reality. But when you awaken in the morning and shake off sleep, you understand that what you experienced as real during the night, was not. In the same way, we have to awaken from material reality as from a bad dream, and open our eyes to the light of unity and the never-ending power of love that is always with us, even though we are unable to see it with our physical eyes.

Illusions can never threaten the truth, just as a nightmare can never threaten the reality we wake up to the next morning. Unfortunately we often give energy and power to illusions, so that in the end they seem to be real. In this way we can be shut out as by a veil from reality. But when the light of truth rises before us, when the illusions fall, we will be able to see and experience the world in a completely different way. We will be able to evaluate what is of importance in the light of God's truth. Only then will we know what true love is, only then will we know what to do to solve fundamental problems on the planet, which is essential for the wellbeing of millions of human destinies:

All the holy Manifestations of God have proclaimed and promulgated the same reality. They have summoned mankind to reality itself, and reality is one. The clouds and mists of imitations have obscured the Sun of Truth. We must forsake these imitations, dispel these clouds and mists and free the Sun from the darkness of superstition. Then will the Sun of Truth shine most gloriously; then all the inhabitants of the world will be united, the religions will be one, sects and denominations will reconcile, all nationalities will flow together in the recognition of one Fatherhood and all degrees of humankind will gather in the shelter of the same tabernacle, under the same banner.[103]

'Abdu'l-Bahá

Many will perhaps be of the opinion that engaging oneself in these thoughts of the unity of humankind is pure philosophy, lacking in practical consequence. But this depends on how we relate to these thoughts. If we become deeply involved in them and pray to be spiritually confirmed in the realization that deep down we are one with all humankind, and that truth is one, we will eventually spontaneously behave differently towards other human beings. To exhibit a willingness to serve, to perform benevolent deeds, to show kindness towards everyone else, no matter of what race, sex, nationality or background, to show love and respect towards all living things, will then be most natural things to do. We will then have an understanding of our place in reality that spontaneously results in new and more loving ways of behaving. We shall look more closely at some of these consequences in the sections to come.

You meet God in all fellow human beings

Thou canst best praise Him if thou lovest His loved ones . . .[104]

Bahá'u'lláh

They whose hearts are warmed by the energizing influence of God's creative love cherish His creatures for His sake, and recognize in every human face a sign of His reflected glory.[105]

Shoghi Effendi

God's love is in everybody, because God has engraved His image in all of us. God's love for God makes God love His image in everybody. When we see God's image in ourselves and in others, we are looking with God's loving glance, with the eye of God. To praise God is to love the ones He loves. Loving Him means loving Him in every face we meet.

> The love which exists between the hearts of believers is prompted by the ideal of the unity of spirits. This love is attained through the knowledge of God, so that men see the Divine Love reflected in the heart. Each sees in the other the Beauty of God reflected in the soul, and finding this point of similarity, they are attracted to one another in love. This love will make all men the waves of one sea, this love will make them all the stars of one heaven and the fruits of one tree. This love will bring the realization of true accord, the foundation of real unity.[106]
>
> *'Abdu'l-Bahá*

Serving a person becomes serving God. If someone asks us to do something, we can in freedom choose to do this as a favour to God. Perhaps we think they ask for something silly, but we do not need to evaluate this. One thing, however, we should reflect upon: if carrying out what the person asks us to do will make us feel humiliated or degraded, we should not do it, for God does not wish the humiliation of His servants. Of course, what is considered humiliation will vary from one person to another. The stronger the consciousness of God's love is rooted in us, the longer the way before the limit of self-degrading humiliation is reached; in this case we can speak of magnanimity and generosity. But in every case we should respect our inner dignity and integrity, for this also means showing respect for the divine potential with which God has invested us. If we transgress these limits and lose our self-respect, we will later experience problems with ourselves, and most likely also with others.

With this in mind, we can see in the following words of Bahá'u-'lláh how He equals doing others a favour with serving God:

> O Son of Man! Deny not My servant should he ask anything from thee, for his face is My face; be then abashed before Me.[107]
>
> *Bahá'u'lláh*

God created you just as equal as everybody else

> Know ye not why We created you all from the same dust? That
> no one should exalt himself over the other. Ponder at all times in
> your hearts how ye were created. Since We have created you all
> from one same substance it is incumbent on you to be even as one
> soul, to walk with the same feet, eat with the same mouth and
> dwell in the same land, that from your inmost being, by your
> deeds and actions, the signs of oneness and the essence of
> detachment may be made manifest. Such is My counsel to you,
> O concourse of light! Heed ye this counsel that ye may obtain the
> fruit of holiness from the tree of wondrous glory.[108]
>
> *Bahá'u'lláh*

No one has the right to put himself above anyone else with regard
to his intrinsic value, for in God's eyes all are, ultimately, equal.
This is our innate birthright: we were all created with pure hearts,
and somewhere within we all still have a fundamental innocence,
a purity and innocence that come from God's Kingdom.

This does not mean that it does not matter what we make of
our lives. God gives us responsibility for managing our talents
well. But it is not our duty to bring others to task for what they
make of their lives:

> Each of us is responsible for one life only, and that is our own.[109]
> *Written on behalf of Shoghi Effendi*

We simply lack the necessary premises to judge other people, and
therefore we should not do so. We can be more gifted in some
respects than others, we may have been more successful in
certain things, but what do we really know about other people's
backgrounds, their potential and their challenges? God has given
every person a task in life; this may differ from one person to
another, and only God knows what it is:

> The whole duty of man in this Day is to attain that share of the
> flood of grace which God poureth forth for him. Let none,
> therefore, consider the largeness or smallness of the receptacle.

75

The portion of some might lie in the palm of a man's hand, the portion of others might fill a cup, and of others even a gallon-measure.[110]

Bahá'u'lláh

Hence, it becomes essential for us under all circumstances to avoid judging others. As individual Bahá'ís we are urged to show each other love, not to judge each other. If anyone is to be punished for violating a basic principle, it is up to the institutions of the Faith, not to you or me. Judging others is not only done by loud pronouncements; it is also common to judge silently. Try to observe what characteristics you give to those to whom you react negatively; before you know what has happened, you may have given them a nick-name, a negative charaterization, or placed them in some kind of psychological category. Psychology is a useful and developing science, but as Bahá'ís it is important to avoid using knowledge of it to put others into categories with a negative charge ("she is so neurotic", "he behaves like a psychopath"). When you attribute such names to others, even if only in your mind, you easily end up considering them as separate from average "normal" human beings, and you easily regard yourself as being better than them. In this way unity is hurt, since others will sense an atmosphere of alienation and condescension. Love is not concerned with categorisation. Love accepts. Love encourages us to forget the "kingdom of names"; by this expression the writings may refer to a way of viewing the world that divides unity into distinctly separate qualities with different names. Love encourages us to see everything with the consciousness of unity, with the eye of the Creator.

Abstaining from comparing ourselves with others becomes important. Of course we may see that we are different with regard to abilities and achievements. But this should not lead us to rank ourselves as generally better or worse than other people. And if we consider ourselves to be worse than others, we are still not in line with the principle of unity that Bahá'u'lláh has laid down. Deep down we are all created equal, neither better nor worse. This has to do with who we are in eternity, seen with God's eye. It has nothing to do with who we have tried to become by being more clever, or by doing more. It is a great relief to realize that the only effort worth making is the effort of gaining a pure heart, and it involves letting go of all ambitions. When the heart is clean, it is the real you who steps forth: your true identity in God's ancient, imperishable and everlasting sovereignty.

> Ever since the seeking of preference and distinction came into play, the world hath been laid waste. It hath become desolate. Those who have quaffed from the ocean of divine utterance and fixed their gaze upon the Realm of Glory should regard themselves as being on the same level as the others and in the same station. Were this matter to be definitely established and conclusively demonstrated through the power and might of God, the world would become as the Abhá Paradise.
>
> Indeed, man is noble, inasmuch as each one is a repository of the sign of God. Nevertheless, to regard oneself as superior in knowledge, learning or virtue, or to exalt oneself or seek preference, is a grievous transgression. Great is the blessedness of those who are adorned with the ornament of this unity and have been graciously confirmed by God.[11]
>
> *Bahá'u'lláh*

Having understood and accepted the principle of unity as the foundation, it may become easier to accept these differences between people, because we see them as secondary. The Bahá'í ideal of "unity in diversity" emphasizes unity, but underlines that unity does not mean uniformity. Unity is a basic quality we are unable to see on the outside; we have to go beyond the physical senses to perceive it. Our physical senses and our minds are trained to register dissimilarities. Hence, we can never hope to achieve complete agreement in all concrete questions. 'Abdu'l-Bahá expresses it like this:

> The differences among the religions of the world are due to the varying types of minds. So long as the powers of the mind are various, it is certain that men's judgments and opinions will differ one from another. If, however, one single, universal perceptive power be introduced – a power encompassing all the rest – those

differing opinions will merge, and a spiritual harmony and oneness will become apparent.[112]

'Abdu'l-Bahá

'Abdu'l-Bahá refers here to a simple, universal power that includes everything else. In another context He refers to this power as the Word of God. We know from the Bahá'í writings that the Word – the Creative Word – is the first thing God created, and this power created the "created world". The Word of God permeates all created things, at the same time as it reveals itself in history through beings such as Buddha, Christ, Muḥammad or Bahá'u'lláh. The words they reveal are also called the Word of God. This subject is explored in more detail in my book *Unlocking the Gate of the Heart*, pages 23–31.

In the following passage 'Abdu'l-Bahá seems to refer to the transcendent power of the Word of God as the unifying force in the universe:

> Naught but the celestial potency of the Word of God, which ruleth and transcendeth the realities of all things, is capable of harmonizing the divergent thoughts, sentiments, ideas, and convictions of the children of men. Verily, it is the penetrating power in all things, the mover of souls and the binder and regulator in the world of humanity.[113]

'Abdu'l-Bahá

To see only the positive in others

One must see in every human being only that which is worthy of praise. When this is done, one can be a friend to the whole human race. If, however, we look at people from the standpoint of their faults, then being a friend to them is a formidable task.

It happened one day in the time of Christ – may the life of the world be a sacrifice unto Him – that He passed by the dead body of a dog, a carcass reeking, hideous, the limbs rotting away. One of those present said: "How foul its stench!" And another said: "How sickening! How loathsome!" To be brief, each one of them had something to add to the list.

But then Christ Himself spoke, and He told them: "Look at that dog's teeth! How gleaming white!"[114]

'Abdu'l-Bahá

A defect has no existence of its own; when the defect is removed it no longer exists. To view defects as real is to make oneself a victim of illusions, since it gives strength to the notion that something that does not exist has a reality. We know that the Bahá'í writings state that evil is the lack of good, just as darkness is the lack of light. When there is light, darkness does not exist. Note that the light does not suppress the darkness, for instance by pressing it into a corner, shoving it away and compressing it so that it can come back later. No, darkness no longer exists at all, when there is light. Light, on the other hand, has no opposite at its level of reality. Light is real because it has an active existence; darkness does not have this. Therefore light is the symbol of the eternal, unchangeable love which no flaw or defect existing on the mortal plane can obstruct. When the light of unity, the light of love, shines, there are no contradictions, because the dark, negative and evil simply do not exist any more. It is exactly the same with regard to the unity deriving from the Abhá Kingdom:

> Spiritual brotherhood may be likened to the light, while the souls of humankind are as lanterns. The incandescent lamps here are many, yet the light is one.[115]

'Abdu'l-Bahá

It is in the material world that our animal nature has its reality. But in relation to God's eternal worlds, the material worlds are not real, they are passing pictures. Humans *are* not really physical bodies, they *are* really eternal souls that in a phase of their eternal existence have put on a physical body. The physical world is in the last analysis an illusion:

> The world is but a show, vain and empty, a mere nothing, bearing the semblance of reality. Set not your affections upon it. Break not the bond that uniteth you with your Creator, and be not of

those that have erred and strayed from His ways. Verily I say, the world is like the vapour in a desert, which the thirsty dreameth to be water and striveth after it with all his might, until when he cometh unto it, he findeth it to be mere illusion. It may, moreover, be likened unto the lifeless image of the beloved whom the lover hath sought and found, in the end, after long search and to his utmost regret, to be such as cannot "fatten nor appease his hunger".[116]

Bahá'u'lláh

Human beings have been endowed with the ability to change the way they perceive the world. We can choose how to see, and what we want to see. Spiritual development is synonymous with changing our view of reality. This ability can of course be misused, but to use it in the service of love is to use it well:

Be in perfect unity. Never become angry with one another . . . Love the creatures for the sake of God and not for themselves. You will never become angry or impatient if you love them for the sake of God. Humanity is not perfect. There are imperfections in every human being, and you will always become unhappy if you look toward the people themselves. But if you look toward God, you will love them and be kind to them, for the world of God is the world of perfection and complete mercy. Therefore, do not look at the shortcomings of anybody; see with the sight of forgiveness. The imperfect eye beholds imperfections. The eye that covers faults looks toward the Creator of souls. He created them, trains and provides for them, endows them with capacity and life, sight and hearing; therefore, they are the signs of His grandeur.[117]

'Abdu'l-Bahá

When 'Abdu'l-Bahá tells us here that we should never be angry with one another, does He really mean that we should repress our anger, walk around with fake smiles and pretend we are friendly? The answer is no. As we are going to see later on, 'Abdu'l-Bahá warns us against hypocrisy. If you are angry, you are angry, whether you express it or not. On the contrary, 'Abdu'l-Bahá says we should not *become* angry. He is suggesting a *different* way of relating, a way that makes this feeling never come into existence. It may of course happen that it comes into existence, and then there are ways we can deal with it. But now we are concerned about not reaching the point where anger arises.

In the passage above 'Abdu'l-Bahá gives us the key for understanding how this can be possible. He asks us to entirely change our perspective. He asks us to acknowledge that *all* people have defects, and that we ourselves will have very unhappy lives if we allow ourselves to become annoyed by everyone else. And now comes what is most important: He asks us to regard people as the Creator regards them. The Creator cares for all people; everyone is a sign of God's creative power. He asks us to turn towards God, meaning towards the light of God's love. It is as He says: Do not look too directly, too hard and inquisitively at others, do not look at the physical person, look towards God's world where everything is perfect, where everything is love. See in your fellow human beings only that which has importance in God's Kingdom. Defects and flaws do not exist there, only the perfect, the loving and the good have any existence there. Every human being has an eternal soul whereon God has engraved His image and His attributes. These attributes are not always so easy to see in the exterior person; and often people are unable to see their good potential qualities themselves. All the more important then that others see them and express that they see them.

One very important point to understand is that friendships based on material circumstances are not lasting friendships, and that only spiritual bonds last:

> The real brotherhood is spiritual, for physical brotherhood is subject to separation. The wars of the outer world of existence separate humankind, but in the eternal world of spiritual brotherhood separation is unknown. Material or physical association is based upon earthly interests, but divine fellowship owes its existence to the breaths of the Holy Spirit.[118]
>
> *'Abdu'l-Bahá*

It is not always easy to love someone one feels disgusted by. In an essay about 'Abdu'l-Bahá, Hand of the Cause George

Townshend tells us how 'Abdu'l-Bahá described how one could look upon others:

> Christ's command to love one's enemies was not obeyed by assuming love nor by acting as though one loved them; for this would be hypocrisy. It was only obeyed when genuine love was felt. When asked how it was possible to love those who were hostile or personally repugnant, He said that love could be true yet indirect. One may love a flower not only for itself but for the sake of someone who sent it. One may love a house because of one who dwells in it. A letter coming from a friend may be precious though the envelope which held it was torn and soiled. So one may love sinners for the sake of the universal Father, and may show kindness to them as to children who need training, to sick persons who need medicine, to wanderers who need guidance. *Treat the sinners, the tyrants, the bloodthirsty enemies as faithful friends and confidants*, He would say. *Consider not their deeds; consider only God.*[119]
>
> George Townshend

It is not always possible to like other people. Luckily we do not have to like everyone personally to practise divine love towards them. It is our love for God, the Father of all, that must be the fundamental emotion when we meet those who are His children:

> We must love God, and in this state, a general love for all men becomes possible. We cannot love each human being for himself, but our feeling towards humanity should be motivated by our love for the Father who created all men.[120]
>
> Written on behalf of Shoghi Effendi

Many think that our emotional reactions to other people cannot be changed, they only come naturally. Modern cognitive psychology has pointed out that this is not the case. Every emotional reaction towards other people contains an interpretation of the situation, an interpretation that is actually made extremely fast. It is possible to learn how to find out what interpretations of the world an emotional reaction is based on, and replace this interpretation with another. This presumes you are willing to observe yourself and learn to know your own reactions, and what are the situations that release them. After a while it will be possible to forestall the reactions. In this way it is possible to learn to interpret surrounding situations in the light of divine love. The interpretations are simple: either someone is asking for love, or they are giving love. Any defect, any provocation, any expression of disgust or hostility is a prayer for love and forgiveness. It is possible to go even one step further: we do not even see the defects, they *are* not, because it is only the power of love, the unifying force in the world, that has any real existence, and its reality is so strong and obvious that everything else loses its meaning in comparison.

> O ye lovers of this wronged one! Cleanse ye your eyes, so that ye behold no man as different from yourselves. See ye no strangers; rather see all men as friends, for love and unity come hard when ye fix your gaze on otherness. And in this new and wondrous age, the Holy Writings say that we must be at one with every people; that we must see neither harshness nor injustice, neither malevolence, nor hostility, nor hate, but rather turn our eyes toward the heaven of ancient glory. For each of the creatures is a sign of God, and it was by the grace of the Lord and His power that each did step into the world; therefore they are not strangers, but in the family; not aliens, but friends, and to be treated as such.[121]
>
> *'Abdu'l-Bahá*

'Abdu'l-Bahá encourages us not to be hypocritical; He regards this as unworthy of a human being.

> Bahá'u'lláh has clearly said in His Tablets that if you have an enemy, consider him not as an enemy. Do not simply be long-suffering; nay, rather, love him. Your treatment of him should be that which is becoming to lovers. Do not even say that he is your enemy. Do not see any enemies: Though he be your murderer, see no enemy. Look upon him with the eye of friendship. Be mindful that you do not consider him as an enemy and simply tolerate

him, for that is but stratagem and hypocrisy. To consider a man your enemy and love him is hypocrisy. This is not becoming of any soul. You must behold him as a friend. You must treat him well. This is right.[122]

'Abdu'l-Bahá

Hypocrisy is a state where a person chooses not to know about emotions he actually has, but does not like. He is denying his own feelings to himself. This can easily happen when one is afraid of not being good enough, or has ambitions to raise oneself above others by showing others a perfect façade. Fanaticism and hypocrisy are closely connected, and the Bahá'í writings strongly encourage us not to be fanatical. 'Abdu'l-Bahá encourages us to be honest with regard to our feelings and to avoid denial and repression. At the same time He shows us a different way of viewing fellow beings, a way that does not give rise to negative feelings, which therefore need not be repressed.

Recognize your enemies as friends, and consider those who wish you evil as the wishers of good. You must not see evil as evil and then compromise with your opinion, for to treat in a smooth, kindly way one whom you consider evil or an enemy is hypocrisy, and this is not worthy or allowable. You must consider your enemies as your friends, look upon your evil-wishers as your well-wishers and treat them accordingly. Act in such a way that your heart may be free from hatred. Let not your heart be offended with anyone.[123]

'Abdu'l-Bahá

To practise love like this implies that we constantly have to concentrate on love, and are conscious of the thoughts we entertain in our mind:

I charge you all that each one of you concentrate all the thoughts of your heart on love and unity. When a thought of war comes, oppose it by a stronger thought of peace. A thought of hatred must be destroyed by a more powerful thought of love. Thoughts of war bring destruction to all harmony, well-being, restfulness and content.

84

Thoughts of love are constructive of brotherhood, peace, friendship, and happiness . . .

If you desire with all your heart, friendship with every race on earth, your thought, spiritual and positive, will spread; it will become the desire of others, growing stronger and stronger, until it reaches the minds of all men.[124]

'Abdu'l-Bahá

"*All* humanity! Every human being! *never forget this*!"

It feels great to have good friends, people who have the same interests as you, the same kind of humour, the same language, the same religion, similar needs. People with common interests find each other and make a small group, a family or a circle of friends. When a new person comes into the circle, the question is whether he "fits into" this circle of friends. If he does not, entrance is denied.

This way of creating groups is human. Everyone needs someone they can relax with and have fun with. Yet creating groups has nothing to do with divine love. Divine love opens itself to absolutely everybody, as we know 'Abdu'l-Bahá did. Therefore we must never mistake the fellowship of common interests for divine love, and we must not let these fellowships stand in the way of our becoming channels for divine love. But having a family, a circle of friends, and fellowship of common interests is not incompatible with practising divine love:

When you love a member of your family or a compatriot, let it be with a ray of the Infinite Love! Let it be in God, and for God! Wherever you find the attributes of God love that person, whether he be of your family or of another. Shed the light of a boundless love on every human being whom you meet, whether of your country, your race, your political party, or of any other nation, colour or shade of political opinion. Heaven will support you while you work in this in-gathering of the scattered peoples of the world beneath the shadow of the almighty tent of unity.

You will be servants of God, who are dwelling near to Him,

His divine helpers in the service, ministering to all Humanity. *All* Humanity! Every human being! *never forget this!*[125]

'Abdu'l-Bahá

People can be fascinated and enchanted by numerous things in this world. They may have a great infatuation for interesting people, for charming people, for gurus and others with special spiritual faculties, for people with extraordinary qualifications in various areas. All these special qualifications have their particular function in some context or another. But when people without special qualifications become uninteresting to befriend, when a person's value is measured in "special" abilities and qualifications, then we are leaving the path of universal love, for this love includes everyone. Admiration for other people's gifts and abilities is not meant to repress the true, universal love. Those who are looking for people who are "special" may well have a self-centred interest in others. But to view oneself as special with regard to others will mean that we have removed ourselves from the recognition of the underlying unity of humanity. We have to be able to give up these vain sides of ourselves, to cleanse our heart for the love that does not emphasize differences in ability, but looks towards the universal and the truly divine in every single human being:

> O Children of Vainglory! For a fleeting sovereignty ye have abandoned My imperishable dominion, and have adorned yourselves with the gay livery of the world and made of it your boast. By My beauty! All will I gather beneath the one-coloured covering of the dust and efface all these diverse colours save them that choose My own, and that is purging from every colour.[126]

Bahá'u'lláh

Having to love every person can seem an inconceivably large task, impossible to master. And this is actually true: it is absolutely impossible to master this without help from something greater than ourselves. The assistance of the Holy Spirit is necessary for us to know what to do. By listening to the voice of truth in the heart, we will come to an idea about "what is the correct and important thing for me to do" in a specific situation. Through the power of the Holy Spirit, an action that may seem outwardly insignificant but is done with true love may have consequences we ourselves cannot see.

You shall not concern yourselves with the mistakes of others

O Son of Being! How couldst thou forget thine own faults and busy thyself with the faults of others? Whoso doeth this is accursed of Me.[127]

Bahá'u'lláh

O Son of Man! Breathe not the sins of others so long as thou art thyself a sinner. Shouldst thou transgress this command, accursed wouldst thou be, and to this I bear witness.[128]

Bahá'u'lláh

To be concerned with the mistakes of others is to give strength to illusions, since mistakes do not have an existence of their own. Actually, you strengthen your own mistakes when you are concerned with the mistakes of others. The more your concern grows, the more you judge others, the harder it will be to see your own mistakes and weaknesses, and thus it becomes increasingly difficult to do something about them. Your condemnation of others turns back to you and becomes your own condemnation. Nothing is more against the law of unity than condemning others, nothing brings on more stagnation in a person's ability to develop spiritually, and nothing can destroy the character and self-respect of a child more than this. Bahá'u'lláh uses very strong words about this. The challenge we are given is to take greater responsibility for our own life and to meddle less in others'. You are only responsible for improving the behaviour of one person, and that is yourself:

If we Bahá'ís cannot attain to cordial unity among ourselves, then we fail to realize the main purpose for which the Báb, Bahá'u'lláh and the Beloved Master lived and suffered.

In order to achieve this cordial unity one of the first essentials insisted on by Bahá'u'lláh and 'Abdu'l-Bahá is that we resist the natural tendency to let our attention dwell on the faults and failings of others rather than on our own. Each of us is responsible for one life only, and that is our own. Each of us is immeasurably far from being "perfect as our heavenly Father is perfect" and the task of perfecting our own life and character is one that requires all our attention, our will-power and energy. If we allow our attention and energy to be taken up in efforts to keep others right and remedy their faults, we are wasting precious time. We are like ploughmen each of whom has his team to manage and his plough to direct, and in order to keep his furrow straight he must keep his eye on his goal and concentrate on his own task. If he looks to this side and that to see how Tom and Harry are getting on and to criticize their ploughing, then his own furrow will assuredly become crooked.

On no subject are the Bahá'í teachings more emphatic than on the necessity to abstain from fault-finding and backbiting while being ever eager to discover and root out our own faults and overcome our own failings.

If we profess loyalty to Bahá'u'lláh, to our Beloved Master and our dear Guardian, then we must show our love by obedience to these explicit teachings. Deeds not words are what they demand, and no amount of fervour in the use of expressions of loyalty and adulation will compensate for failure to live in the spirit of the teachings.[129]

Written on behalf of Shoghi Effendi

To concern your thoughts with other people's mistakes is bad enough. If you also share these thoughts with others, the negative effect will increase. Slander and backbiting, that is, discussing other people's mistakes and weaknesses, create negative attitudes that influence those who are listening and make it more difficult for them to see those discussed as they really are, and accept them in the light of God's love.

I hope that the believers of God will shun completely backbiting, each one praising the other cordially and believe that *backbiting is the cause of Divine wrath*, to such an extent that if a person backbites to the extent of one word, he may become dishonoured among all the people, because the most hateful characteristic of man is fault-finding. One must expose the praiseworthy qualities of the souls and not their evil attributes. The friends must overlook their shortcomings and faults and speak only of their virtues and not their defects.[130]

'Abdu'l-Bahá

We must do our best not to allow ourselves to talk badly about others. Yet we should not become passive listeners when someone is slandering another. 'Abdu'l-Bahá explains how in a friendly manner we can interfere to change such a situation:

O beloved of the Lord! If any soul speak ill of an absent one, the only result will clearly be this: he will dampen the zeal of the friends and tend to make them indifferent. For backbiting is divisive, it is the leading cause among the friends of a disposition to withdraw. If any individual should speak ill of one who is absent, it is incumbent on his hearers, in a spiritual and friendly manner, to stop him, and say in effect: would this detraction serve any useful purpose? Would it please the Blessed Beauty, contribute to the lasting honour of the friends, promote the holy Faith, support the Covenant, or be of any possible benefit to any soul? No, never! On the contrary, it would make the dust to settle so thickly on the heart that the ears would hear no more, and the eyes would no longer behold the light of truth.

If, however, a person setteth about speaking well of another, opening his lips to praise another, he will touch an answering chord in his hearers and they will be stirred up by the breathings of God.[131]

'Abdu'l-Bahá

The role of peace-maker is important within the Bahá'í community too:

What the believers need is not only, as you state, to really study the teachings, but also to have more peace-makers circulating among them. Unfortunately, not only average people, but average Bahá'ís, are very immature; gossip, trouble-making, criticism, seem easier than the putting into practice of love, constructive words and cooperation. It is one of the functions of the older and the more mature Bahá'ís, to help the weaker ones to iron out their difficulties and learn to really function and live like true believers![132]

Written on behalf of Shoghi Effendi

When problems with exaggerated criticism and slander arise in a community, it is not necessarily always a good solution to point out the mistake. To criticize others for criticising is after all to commit the same mistake that you are trying to correct. The only thing you can safely do then is to try to behave correctly yourself:

Human frailties and peculiarities can be a great test. But the only way, or perhaps I should say the first and best way, to remedy such situations is to oneself do what is right. One soul can be the cause of the spiritual illumination of a continent. Now that you have seen, and remedied a great fault in your own life, now that you see more clearly what is lacking in your own community, there is nothing to prevent you from arising and showing such an example, such a love and spirit of service, as to enkindle the hearts of your fellow Bahá'ís.

He urges you to study deeply the teachings, teach others, study with those Bahá'ís who are anxious to do so the deeper teachings of our Faith, and through example, effort and prayer bring about a change.[133]

Written on behalf of Shoghi Effendi

Many seem to believe that the prohibition of backbiting only concerns situations when untruthful statements are made about others. This is not the case. Any mentioning of faults or negative characteristics of other people is backbiting, and is not allowed:

Even if what is said against another person be true, the mentioning of his faults to others still comes under the category of backbiting, and is forbidden.[134]

Written on behalf of Shoghi Effendi

Backbiting often happens when one is frustrated, wounded or infuriated by the behaviour of another person. When you are in such a mood you will feel a need to "empty yourself" in order to get rid of these unpleasant feelings. The Universal House of Justice has given guidance in a letter to an individual on how to deal with such situations:

> You ask in your letter for guidance on the implications of the prohibition on backbiting and more specifically whether, in moments of anger or depression, the believer is permitted to turn to his friends to unburden his soul and discuss his problem in human relations. Normally, it is possible to describe the situation surrounding a problem and seek help and advice in resolving it, without necessarily mentioning names. The individual believer should seek to do this, whether he is consulting a friend, Bahá'í or non-Bahá'í, or whether the friend is consulting him.
>
> 'Abdu'l-Bahá does not permit adverse criticism of individuals by name in discussion among the friends, even if the one criticizing believes that he is doing so to protect the interests of the Cause. If the situation is of such gravity as to endanger the interests of the Faith, the complaint, as your National Spiritual Assembly has indicated, should be submitted to the Local Spiritual Assembly, or as you state to a representative of the institution of the Counsellors, for consideration and action. In such cases, of course, the name of the person or persons involved will have to be mentioned.
>
> You also ask what one should do to "handle depression and anger with someone" one feels "very positively about". The Universal House of Justice suggests that you call to mind the admonitions found in our Writings on the need to overlook the shortcomings of others, to forgive and conceal their misdeeds, not to expose their bad qualities, but to search for and affirm their praiseworthy ones, and endeavour to be always forbearing, patient and merciful.[135]
>
> *The Universal House of Justice*

Look at your own challenges, not at other people's mistakes

Not being concerned with the mistakes of others, but concentrating on working on our own, is an important method of avoiding the spreading of negativity and alienation. To work on our own mistakes does not mean we should condemn ourselves, becoming introverted and depressive. In order to start the work of improving ourselves it is enough in the first instance to earnestly admit to ourselves that we have made a mistake. It is not productive to use the knowledge of our own mistakes to beat ourselves over the head, feeling unworthy, becoming chronically ashamed, filled with guilt and regarding ourselves as worse than others. Rather, we need to find a place in ourselves where we are able to observe ourselves in an active and attentive way, without condemning or being disgusted, and at the same time without indulging in self-satisfaction. If we are able to observe ourselves in this way, we are also able to accept ourselves and our own emotions, and we then have the best starting point for changing ourselves. When we are able to accept our own weaknesses without repulsion, it will become much easier to accept the weaknesses of other people and provide them with the love they need.

Turning our attention towards ourselves and our own mistakes and challenges is a useful tool when dealing with situations where we are tempted to concern ourselves with other people's mistakes:

> As to backbiting, the House of Justice points out that learning not to concern oneself with the faults of others seems to be one of the most difficult lessons for people to master, and that failing in this is a fertile cause of disputes among the Bahá'ís as it is among men and women in general. In "Star of the West", Volume 8, No. 10, on page 138, there is a record of a reply given by 'Abdu'l-Bahá in a private interview in Paris in 1913. He was asked "How shall I overcome seeing the faults of others – recognizing the wrong in others?", and He replied: "I will tell you. Whenever you recognize the fault of another, think of yourself! What are my imperfections? – and try to remove them. Do this whenever you

are tried through the words or deeds of others. Thus you will grow, become more perfect. You will overcome self, you will not even have time to think of the faults of others . . ."[136]

The Universal House of Justice

When discussing the principle of the Holy Spirit, it was pointed out earlier in this book how important it is not to look at our own limitations and weaknesses, while in the present context we are exhorted to do so. These instructions may seem incompatible, but actually they are not. The material person is limited to time and space, and is therefore to a certain degree powerless. To know ourselves and our body is useful in situations such as those mentioned above: because here we need contact with the earth, we need to limit ourselves with regard to others so that we do not become involved with their negative sides, we need to centre ourselves in our own heart. 'Abdu'l-Bahá describes a way not to lose your head, a sort of composure that is necessary so that our lower self cannot carry us away; this involves an acknowledgement of our powerlessness, our poverty in a given situation. When in the daily obligatory prayer we bear witness to our own weakness and poverty, we are possibly testifying to the limitations of our physical selves. This also enables us to do the opposite: to testify to God's strength and wealth. The strength and wealth we refer to are not our own, but they are at our disposition when we summon them. What we refer to, therefore, is the power of the Holy Spirit that gives us knowledge about things we have not learned, and love where our personal ability to love falls short. If we now were to limit ourselves only to see ourselves as material creatures, we would not be able to utilize this power. We would limit our radius to what we can reach physically. Therefore we also need the ability to forget ourselves and our limitations and trust that God's Concourse on High will inspire and guide us when we arise to serve Him.

To not offend, nor let yourself be offended

When we feel offended, it is our animal nature that is hurt. A wounded animal is dangerous – it longs to share its pain with others. When we hurt others, it is our animal nature that does so. The Bahá'í writings encourage us strongly to avoid hurting others, and not to let ourselves be hurt. They encourage us not to take revenge, not to "pay back".

> Should anyone wax angry with you, respond to him with gentleness; and should anyone upbraid you, forbear to upbraid him in return, but leave him to himself and put your trust in God, the omnipotent Avenger, the Lord of might and justice.[137]
>
> *Bahá'u'lláh*

> O army of God! Beware lest ye harm any soul, or make any heart to sorrow; lest ye wound any man with your words, be he known to you or a stranger, be he friend or foe. Pray ye for all; ask ye that all be blessed, all be forgiven. Beware, beware, lest any of you seek vengeance, even against one who is thirsting for your blood. Beware, beware, lest ye offend the feelings of another, even though he be an evil-doer, and he wish you ill. Look ye not upon the creatures, turn ye to their Creator. See ye not the never-yielding people, see but the Lord of Hosts. Gaze ye not down upon the dust, gaze upward at the shining sun, which hath caused every patch of darksome earth to glow with light.[138]
>
> *'Abdu'l-Bahá*

It may be a challenge to restrain oneself from letting all the acid go when one is really furious. A challenge just as serious can be to not let yourself be hurt, without protecting yourself in ways that make the problem worse. It can be of help to remember that the one who hurts someone else usually feels hurt or threatened himself, perhaps not even by you, but by someone else. If you are able to see the helplessness and vulnerability of the person offending you, if you understand that what he is saying to hurt you actually does not concern you, you may then be able to feel sorry for this vulnerable and frightened person, and not see yourself as being attacked.

Another important consideration is that only God may judge people; no one else has the right to do so. Therefore you should not be affected by another person's judgement of you, as if it were entirely true or just. If you do so, you are putting your fellow human beings in God's place:

> Trust in God, and be unmoved by either praise or false accusations . . . depend entirely on God.[139]
>
> *'Abdu'l-Bahá*

> Set before thine eyes God's unerring Balance and, as one standing in His Presence, weigh in that Balance thine actions every day, every moment of thy life. Bring thyself to account ere thou art summoned to a reckoning . . .[140]
>
> *Bahá'u'lláh*

Other people may have many reasons to point out your mistakes and find your weak spots. We know that the need to point out the mistakes of others usually derives from our lower, animal self. There is clear encouragement in the writings not to let oneself be affected by false accusations. Your reference for what is wrong and right are the Holy Writings, and nothing else. That others are concerned with your defects and mistakes is something you should not make your problem; it is actually their own problem. We should not encourage anyone to be concerned with the mistakes of others by letting them rule us through creating feelings of guilt in us. If you are sure that God loves you, the accusations made by others will not affect you. If you defend yourself, it means you feel attacked. Defence is counter-attack. Defence gives strength to the idea that defects are real and have an existence, while the opposite is the case in spiritual matters.

It is easy to use the knowledge that you have made a mistake to hurt yourself by punishing yourself too harshly. This will then affect both you and others negatively. If you know you have the tendency to punish yourself too harshly, you have to be on guard not to let negative ways of thinking develop in your mind. You have, for instance, made a mistake. If you acknowledge this, and decide to do something better next time, fine. But if you tell yourself what an idiot you must be, and curse yourself, you are starting an attack on yourself that may build up and throw you at last into deep depression. You should be prepared to stop vicious circles like this. As soon as you sense you are on that track, you have to tell yourself firmly that while you recognise that you have made a mistake, it is not the will of God for you to condemn yourself, because God believes you are created noble. You can then call on God's name and for a moment forget everything except Him.

If you get hurt, which is only human, it is important to be alert. You are in a situation where you can learn a lot about yourself, about your reactions and your relation to fellow human beings. You can calmly observe what it is like to be hurt (perhaps a burning feeling in the chest . . .an impulse to hit back . . . to take revenge . . . to draw back, etc.). If you engage your attention in learning about yourself and your reactions, you are doing exactly what 'Abdu'l-Bahá wishes you to do in such a situation: to direct your gaze towards yourself, towards your mistakes, instead of hitting back at someone else. The intention to learn in every situation thereby becomes the key to a more loving conduct.

See Bahá'u'lláh standing before you

It is Our wish and desire that every one of you may become a source of all goodness unto men, and an example of uprightness to mankind. Beware lest ye prefer yourselves above your neighbours. Fix your gaze upon Him Who is the Temple of God amongst men. He, in truth, hath offered up His life as a ransom for the redemption of the world. He, verily, is the All-Bountiful, the Gracious, the Most High. If any differences arise amongst you, behold Me standing before your face, and overlook the faults of one another for My name's sake and as a token of your love for My manifest and resplendent Cause. We love to see you at all times consorting in amity and concord within the paradise of My good-pleasure, and to inhale from your acts the fragrance of friendliness and unity, of loving-kindness and fellowship. Thus counselleth you the All-Knowing, the Faithful. We shall always be with you . . .[141]

Bahá'u'lláh

In this text, Bahá'u'lláh gives us very important advice to practise and use:

96

If any differences arise amongst you, behold Me standing before your face, and overlook the faults of one another for My name's sake, and as a token of your love for My manifest and resplendent Cause.

Composure is important when we find ourselves in a situation of conflict, a situation where there are strong differences of opinion. Composure may consist in stopping for a moment, taking a deep breath, and stating for ourselves what is about to happen. If we have managed to compose ourselves, we can practise using Bahá'u'lláh's advice: to see Him standing before us. If Bahá'u'lláh or 'Abdu'l-Bahá were present in the room, what would you say, how would you express yourself? Listen to your own spirit, not only the words of the other person or your own feelings or plans to attack. What does the Holy Spirit have to say? What advice can you imagine 'Abdu'l-Bahá would give you? If you can manage this form of composure and prayer in the actual situation, you will soon experience that the Holy Spirit is with you and ready to help you in all situations where you are unable to cope on your own.

Bahá'u'lláh also gives us some advice on how to quench the "flame of hatred" in a given situation. The key is once again composure, and to remind ourselves of some words revealed by Him. He tells us:

Say: O servants! Let not the means of order be made the cause of confusion and the instrument of union an occasion for discord. We fain would hope that the people of Bahá may be guided by the blessed words: "Say: all things are of God." This exalted utterance is like unto water for quenching the fire of hate and enmity which smouldereth within the hearts and breasts of men. By this single utterance contending peoples and kindreds will attain the light of true unity. Verily He speaketh the truth and leadeth the way. He is the All-Powerful, the Exalted, the Gracious.[142]

Bahá'u'lláh

To encompass the frailty of others with tender care

Now must the lovers of God arise to carry out these instructions of His: let them be kindly fathers to the children of the human race, and compassionate brothers to the youth, and self-denying offspring to those bent with years. The meaning of this is that ye must show forth tenderness and love to every human being, even to your enemies, and welcome them all with unalloyed friendship, good cheer, and loving-kindness. When ye meet with cruelty and persecution at another's hands, keep faith with him; when malevolence is directed your way, respond with a friendly heart. To the spears and arrows rained upon you, expose your breasts for a target mirror-bright; and in return for curses, taunts and wounding words, show forth abounding love. Thus will all peoples witness the power of the Most Great Name, and every nation acknowledge the might of the Ancient Beauty, and see how He hath toppled down the walls of discord, and how surely He hath guided all the peoples of the earth to oneness; how He hath lit man's world, and made this earth of dust to send forth streams of light.

These human creatures are even as children, they are brash and unconcerned. These children must be reared with infinite, loving care, and tenderly fostered in the embraces of mercy, so that they may taste the spiritual honey-sweetness of God's love; that they may become like unto candles shedding their beams across this darksome world, and may clearly perceive what blazing crowns of glory the Most Great Name, the Ancient Beauty, hath set on the brows of His beloved, what bounties He hath bestowed on the hearts of those He holdeth dear, what a love He hath cast into the breasts of humankind, and what treasures of friendship He hath made to appear amongst all men.[143]

'Abdu'l-Bahá

There are many ways to react when we experience that others do something wrong, act in a provocative manner or with evil intent. 'Abdu'l-Bahá encourages us to meet attitudes like these with friendliness. This is only possible for someone who is already as an eternal being, who cannot be threatened or offended by anything

98

in the material world. He asks us to look with concern on those who are evil. He wants us to look at them as children who have gone astray, not as opposition or threats. We know that God loves all people, and 'Abdu'l-Bahá has given us His own example of how the love He talks about here can be lived. To live like this is only possible with the help of the Holy Spirit. 'Abdu'l-Bahá's spirit is alive and is there, to be of continuous help and inspiration for us. In the prayer that ends the text we have quoted above, 'Abdu'l-Bahá expresses the hope that the heavenly legions will give us guidance so that we are able to do what He has described:

> O God, my God! Aid Thou Thy trusted servants to have loving and tender hearts. Help them to spread, amongst all the nations of the earth, the light of guidance that cometh from the Company on high. Verily Thou art the Strong, the Powerful, the Mighty, the All-Subduing, the Ever-Giving. Verily Thou art the Generous, the Gentle, the Tender, the Bountiful.[144]
>
> *'Abdu'l-Bahá*

Justice and love

Every civilized society has to lay down certain rules for what individuals are allowed to do to others and to society itself. These rules are formulated in laws. In order to train people to keep to these laws, society introduces punishment for certain violations. In earlier societies, punishment and revenge were nearly the same: if someone outside the clan had committed a crime against someone in the clan, the clan was given the authority to punish the violator or his clan. The punishment was therefore emotionally motivated: there were motives of revenge behind it. The clan that now suffered revenge would often wish to revenge itself in turn. The result could be century-long feuds. Societies like these had bad conditions for love and forgiveness.

The introduction of the rule of law solved this problem: a police force and a judiciary that had no motive of revenge took care of punishment. Punishment became no longer a responsibility resting on individuals. Hence, each individual was free to practise benevolence and forgiveness.

This model for sorting out matters of justice and love is continued in the social order the Bahá'ís are working to create. Most of the questions that have to do with setting limits, and reprimand and everything that has to do with punishment, are referred to the institutions that are named Houses of Justice in the Bahá'í writings. At present these are represented by the Universal House of Justice, which is the highest institution in the Bahá'í community, and by the National and Local Spiritual Assemblies. As individuals the Bahá'ís are therefore free to practise full acceptance, forgiveness and love towards others. At the same time we have to accept that the assemblies are responsible for setting limits. Many problems in the Bahá'í community are due to misunderstandings concerning this division of labour:

> There is a tendency to mix up the functions of the Administration and try to apply it in individual relationships, which is abortive, because the Assembly is a nascent House of Justice and is supposed to administer, according to the Teachings, the affairs of the community. But individuals towards each other are governed by love, unity, forgiveness and a sin-covering eye. Once the friends grasp this they will get along much better, but they keep playing Spiritual Assembly to each other and expect the Assembly to behave like an individual . . .[145]
>
> *Written on behalf of Shoghi Effendi*

Of course there are situations where one wishes to give advice to others, where one feels it is one's duty to tell someone that things should be done in another way. The case may not be so serious that it should be referred to an Assembly, yet you feel it would be right to correct someone. In cases like these, the Bahá'í writings emphasize that instruction should be given in a very kind way. The one who gives the guidance should not regard himself as better than the other. If the motive is to teach the other a lesson – a motive of revenge – such a thing is in accordance with the laws of neither love nor justice.

Show forbearance and benevolence and love to one another. Should any one among you be incapable of grasping a certain truth, or be striving to comprehend it, show forth, when conversing with him, a spirit of extreme kindliness and good-will. Help him to see and recognize the truth, without esteeming yourself to be, in the least, superior to him, or to be possessed of greater endowments.[146]

Bahá'u'lláh

Consort with all men, O people of Bahá, in a spirit of friendliness and fellowship. If ye be aware of a certain truth, if ye possess a jewel, of which others are deprived, share it with them in a language of utmost kindliness and good-will. If it be accepted, if it fulfil its purpose, your object is attained. If any one should refuse it, leave him unto himself, and beseech God to guide him. Beware lest ye deal unkindly with him. A kindly tongue is the lodestone of the hearts of men. It is the bread of the spirit, it clotheth the words with meaning, it is the fountain of the light of wisdom and understanding . . .[147]

Bahá'u'lláh

To forgive others

Let not your heart be offended with anyone. If some one commits an error and wrong toward you, you must instantly forgive him.[148]

'Abdu'l-Bahá.

Divine love demands that we are willing to love all people. This power of love is blocked if your relation to another person is influenced by resentment, bitterness or the desire for vengeance. Divine love does not make any exceptions. That is why you cannot make exceptions either, if you wish to be a channel for the divine power of love. Being a channel means you are receiving the power yourself. If you withhold it from others, you also withhold it from yourself. You deprive yourself of love by withholding it from others. To forgive others becomes essential, since it means opening the channel of love both for yourself and others.

The signs that you have not forgiven another person can be many: the obvious signs are rage, hatred, anger, bitterness, resentment, contempt and arrogance. Other signs can be more difficult to discover: withdrawal (meaning the wish to have nothing to do with the person), malicious pleasure or depression. Forgiving others is not denying these emotions or pretending they do not exist. It is something more than just saying you forgive the person. Forgiveness goes deeper, it demands that your feelings forget what has occurred, so that you no longer nurture hatred or bitterness towards the person concerned. We cannot force ourselves to forgive; this often becomes artificial and does not reach the depth of the problem.

Some important steps in the practice of forgiveness are:

- to accept the emotions, i.e. make friends with your bad feelings, so that you do not push them away or project them onto others;

- put away the thoughts of what happened;

- fully and wholly turn towards God and pray for His love and mercy, and forget everything except Him.

If you can manage this, you will sooner or later experience what was done to you as a trifling matter, as nothing compared to the joy and peace that shines from God's sun of love.

To forgive can in serious cases be a process that takes years to complete. Just starting the process and wanting to work with it will attract the divine power of love to you, and this is exactly what you need. It will help you mend your self-esteem. It is not possible to fully forgive someone if you keep regarding yourself as a victim, or see yourself surrounded by enemies. The only way to go is that of divine love, and we must be willing to let go our enemy-pictures, and to view all the tests we may encounter as given to us so that we can learn from them and grow from them. Of course, God does not wish anyone to hurt another. Yet if it happens anyway, some responsibility rests on the person who is hurt to use what has happened to grow. When we sincerely wish it, the Concourse on High will assist us, and we will at last be able to forgive completely. If we are left to walk around in resentment, we will hurt others, even without consciously wanting to, and we will ourselves be shut out from the kingdom of unity.

Love is now. Not to forgive is to let something that happened in the past, and that no longer exists, to hinder us from experiencing love here and now. To put the past behind us is the central consideration here. God's love is with you now, in this very moment when you are reading this, and will be with you every single moment you are alive and in all the worlds thereafter. To forgive others is to give yourself the opportunity of receiving the gift of love that is with us from eternity to eternity.

> We must never dwell too much on the attitudes and feelings of our fellow-believers towards us. What is most important is to foster love and harmony and ignore any rebuffs we may receive; in this way the weaknesses of human nature and the peculiarity or attitude of any particular person is not magnified, but pales into insignificance in comparison with our joint service to the Faith we all love.[149]
>
> *Written on behalf of Shoghi Effendi*

Everyone seeks the truth

Two people can experience the same thing in entirely different ways. People from different cultures have very different ways of thinking and of experiencing the world. To give an example: a rainbow is an optical phenomenon with an entirely continuous transition between nuances of colour. In our culture, however, we have separated it into seven dissimilar, separate steps, and when we look at it, it seems as though it actually is divided in this way. People from other cultures have organised this experience differently. In some cultures, green and blue, for instance, are considered to be the same colour. In other cultures, yellow and red are seen as one. People from these cultures will experience what they see with their eyes accordingly. But despite these dissimilarities in perception, reality – the rainbow – is one.

This is exactly how it is with people's different perceptions of truth. Truth – which is the real, deep reality – is one, but different people have different perceptions of it and approach it differently.

This is important to understand, so that seeming differences do not make us lose sight of the fundamental unity.

> . . . when you meet those whose opinions differ from your own, do not turn away your face from them. All are seeking truth, and there are many roads leading thereto. Truth has many aspects, but it remains always and forever one.
>
> Do not allow difference of opinion, or diversity of thought to separate you from your fellow-men, or to be the cause of dispute, hatred and strife in your hearts.
>
> Rather, search diligently for the truth and make all men your friends.[150]

'Abdu'l-Bahá

TO GIVE LASTING HAPPINESS TO   8
OTHERS

The Faith of the Blessed Beauty is summoning mankind to safety and love, to amity and peace; it hath raised up its tabernacle on the heights of the earth, and directeth its call to all nations. Wherefore, O ye who are God's lovers, know ye the value of this precious Faith, obey its teachings, walk in this road that is drawn straight, and show ye this way to the people. Lift up your voices and sing out the song of the Kingdom. Spread far and wide the precepts and counsels of the loving Lord, so that this world will change into another world, and this darksome earth will be flooded with light, and the dead body of mankind will arise and live; so that every soul will ask for immortality, through the holy breaths of God.[51]

'Abdu'l-Bahá

Love is a light that shines in the darkness. Our task is to reflect this light, so that those who are in darkness can take part in the light. Love is everlasting happiness, and this happiness is closely connected with faith in God. When we have gained access to this happiness and experienced it in our lives, we want of course to share it with others, because sharing lies in the nature of love. Love grows when shared with others.

The greatest thing we can do in our lives is to guide another person to the source of eternal happiness and love:

It is better to guide one soul than to possess all that is on earth, for as long as that guided soul is under the shadow of the Tree of Divine Unity, he and the one who hath guided him will both be recipients of God's tender mercy, whereas possession of earthly things will cease at the time of death. The path to guidance is one of love and compassion, not of force and coercion. This hath been God's method in the past, and shall continue to be in the future! He causeth him whom He pleaseth to enter the shadow of His Mercy. Verily, He is the Supreme Protector, the All-Generous.

There is no paradise more wondrous for any soul than to be exposed to God's Manifestation in His Day, to hear His verses and believe in them, to attain His presence, which is naught but the presence of God, to sail upon the sea of the heavenly kingdom of His good-pleasure, and to partake of the choice fruits of the paradise of His divine Oneness.[152]

The Báb

Love and true happiness can be spread in many ways:

In this day, the one favoured at the Threshold of the Lord is he who handeth round the cup of faithfulness; who bestoweth, even upon his enemies, the jewel of bounty, and lendeth, even to his fallen oppressor, a helping hand; it is he who will, even to the fiercest of his foes, be a loving friend. These are the Teachings of the Blessed Beauty, these the counsels of the Most Great Name. . .

Soon will your swiftly-passing days be over, and the fame and riches, the comforts, the joys provided by this rubbish-heap, the world, will be gone without a trace. Summon ye, then, the people to God, and invite humanity to follow the example of the Company on high. Be ye loving fathers to the orphan, and a refuge to the helpless, and a treasury for the poor, and a cure for the ailing. Be ye the helpers of every victim of oppression, the patrons of the disadvantaged. Think ye at all times of rendering some service to every member of the human race. Pay ye no heed to aversion and rejection, to disdain, hostility, injustice: act ye in the opposite way. Be ye sincerely kind, not in appearance only. Let each one of God's loved ones centre his attention on this: to be the Lord's mercy to man; to be the Lord's grace. Let him do some good to every person whose path he crosseth, and be of some benefit to him. Let him improve the character of each and all, and reorient the minds of men. In this way, the

TO GIVE LASTING HAPPINESS TO OTHERS

light of divine guidance will shine forth, and the blessings of God will cradle all mankind: for love is light, no matter in what abode it dwelleth; and hate is darkness, no matter where it may make its nest. O friends of God! That the hidden Mystery may stand revealed, and the secret essence of all things may be disclosed, strive ye to banish that darkness for ever and ever.[153]

'Abdu'l-Bahá

When the flame of God's true love is lit in a heart, its influence will spread. This influence is not limited to people's material radius, their physical sphere of action; the effects of it will be noticed both in East and West, and in God's invisible worlds. We should not, therefore, underestimate the significance of coming into contact with this dimension, neither with regard to ourselves nor with regard to others.

O living flame of heavenly love! Thine heart hath been so fired with the love of God that from ten thousand leagues afar its warmth and radiance may be felt and seen. The fire lit by mortal hand imparteth light and warmth to but a little space, whereas that sacred flame which the Hand of God hath kindled, though burning in the east, will set aflame the west and give warmth to both the north and the south; nay, it shall rise from this world to glow with the hottest flame in the realms on high, flooding with light the Kingdom of eternal glory.

Happy art thou to have obtained so heavenly a gift. Blessed art thou to be favoured with His divine bestowals.

The glory of God rest upon thee and upon them that hold fast unto the sure handle of His Will and holy Covenant.[154]

'Abdu'l-Bahá

Humankind, however, needs a new social order, and we Bahá'ís are working to establish it. Yet at the same time most people have an intense need to be granted access to true love. Active understanding and acceptance is something we can offer every person we meet:

The people of the world not only need the laws and principles of the Bahá'í Faith – they desperately need to see the love that is

engendered by it in the hearts of its followers, and to partake of that atmosphere of tolerance, understanding, forbearance and active kindness which should be the hall-mark of a Bahá'í Community.[155]
Written on behalf of Shoghi Effendi

The Bahá'í community is a place where people are supposed to meet universal love. The unity of the Bahá'í community is therefore an essential foundation for teaching others about the Faith.

> Today the one overriding need is unity and harmony among the beloved of the Lord, for they should have among them but one heart and soul and should, so far as in them lieth, unitedly withstand the hostility of all the peoples of the world; they must bring to an end the benighted prejudices of all nations and religions and must make known to every member of the human race that all are the leaves of one branch, the fruits of one bough.
> Until such time, however, as the friends establish perfect unity among themselves, how can they summon others to harmony and peace?[156]
>
> *'Abdu'l-Bahá*

Unity in the Bahá'í community thus becomes an important basis for sharing true love with others. Many of the prerequisites for doing this have already been discussed. Some special cases are explored in the following section.

Unity in the Bahá'í community

The Bahá'í community is a place where people meet who would not normally choose each other's company. As such, it is the perfect place to train oneself in the practise of divine love. The challenges can be many. It is therefore important to be aware of some guidelines that will help us tackle the differences in opinion and the tests that will occur as a natural part of the growth of this diverse community.

- Discussions about the correct interpretation of the Bahá'í writings should be referred to the institutions of the Faith, in the last instance to the Universal House of Justice. As individuals we of course have the opportunity and are encouraged to make our own private interpretations of the writings. It is when questions arise on behalf of the Bahá'í community as such that we should seek an authoritative answer.

In brief, O ye believers of God! The text of the divine Book is this: If two souls quarrel and contend about a question of the divine questions, differing and disputing, both are wrong. The wisdom of this incontrovertible law of God is this: That between two souls from amongst the believers of God, no contention and dispute may arise; that they may speak with each other with infinite amity and love. Should there appear the least trace of controversy, they must remain silent, and both parties must continue their discussions no longer, but ask the reality of the question from the Interpreter. This is the irrefutable command!¹⁵⁷

'Abdu'l-Bahá

• The roles of the individual and the administration should not be confused.

Love is the standard which must govern the conduct of one believer towards another. The administrative order does not change this, but unfortunately sometimes the friends confuse the two, and try to be a whole spiritual assembly, – with the discipline and justice and impartiality that body must show, – to each other, instead of being forgiving, loving and patient to each other as individuals.¹⁵⁸

Written on behalf of Shoghi Effendi

• New Bahá'í communities should not be over-administered.

He urges you to do all you can to promote unity and love amongst the members of the Community there, as this seems to be their greatest need.

So often young communities, in their desire to administer the Cause, lose sight of the fact that these spiritual relationships are far more important and fundamental than the rules and regulations which must govern the conduct of community affairs.[159]

Written on behalf of Shoghi Effendi

- Put the past behind you.

When criticism and harsh words arise within a Bahá'í community, there is no remedy except to put the past behind one, and persuade all concerned to turn over a new leaf, and for the sake of God and His Faith refrain from mentioning the subjects which have led to misunderstanding and inharmony. The more the friends argue back and forth and maintain, each side, that their point of view is the right one, the worse the whole situation becomes.

When we see the condition the world is in today, we must surely forget these utterly insignificant internal disturbances, and rush, unitedly, to the rescue of humanity. You should urge your fellow-Bahá'ís to take this point of view, and to support you in a strong effort to suppress every critical thought and every harsh word, in order to let the spirit of Bahá'u'lláh flow into the entire community, and unite it in His love and in His service.[160]

Written on behalf of Shoghi Effendi

- The Nineteen Day Feast is held to create unity and solidarity.

The Nineteen Day Feast was inaugurated by the Báb and ratified by Bahá'u'lláh, in His holy book, the Aqdas, so that people may gather together and outwardly show fellowship and love, that the divine mysteries may be disclosed. The object is concord, that through this fellowship hearts may become perfectly united, and reciprocity and mutual helpfulness be established.[161]

'Abdu'l-Bahá

You must continue to keep the Nineteen Day Feast. It is very important; it is very good. But when you present yourselves in the meetings, before entering them, free yourselves from all that you have in your heart, free your thoughts and your minds from all else save God, and speak to your heart. That all may make this a gathering of love, make it the cause of illumination, make it a gathering of attraction of the hearts, surround this gathering with the Lights of the Supreme Concourse, so that you may be gathered together with the utmost love.[162]

'Abdu'l-Bahá

- Encourage, do not criticize.

The Guardian believes that a great deal of the difficulties from which the believers . . . feel themselves to be suffering are caused by their neither correctly understanding nor putting into practice the administration. They seem – many of them – to be prone to continually challenging and criticizing the decisions of their Assemblies. If the Bahá'ís undermine the very bodies which are, however immaturely, seeking to co-ordinate Bahá'í activities and administer Bahá'í affairs, if they continually criticize their acts and challenge or belittle their decisions, they not only prevent any real rapid progress in the Faith's development from taking place, but they repel outsiders who quite rightly may ask how we ever expect to unite the whole world when we are so disunited among ourselves!

There is only one remedy for this: to study the administration, to obey the Assemblies, and each believer seek to perfect his *own* character as a Bahá'í. We can never exert the influence over others which we can exert over ourselves. If we are better, if we show love, patience, and understanding of the weaknesses of others; if we seek to never criticize but rather encourage, others will do likewise, and we can really help the Cause through our example and spiritual strength. The Bahá'ís everywhere, when the administration is first established, find it very difficult to adjust themselves. They have to learn to obey, even when the Assembly may be wrong, for the sake of *unity*. They have to sacrifice their personalities, to a certain extent, in order that the community life may grow and develop as a whole. These things are difficult – but we must realize that they will lead us to a very much greater, more perfect, way of life when the Faith is properly established according to the administration.[163]

Written on behalf of Shoghi Effendi

• Universal participation.

> The real secret of universal participation lies in the Master's oft expressed wish that the friends should love each other, constantly encourage each other, work together, be as one soul in one body . . .[164]
>
> *The Universal House of Justice*

To teach the Cause is to spread love

> If between the friends true love – based on the love of God – could become manifest, the Cause would spread very rapidly.[165]
>
> *Written on behalf of Shoghi Effendi*

To teach others about the Bahá'í Faith is to pass on the flame of love. We are not involved in persuading, but in giving them contact with the source of love. We are not asking them for anything, but offering the greatest gift.

> O friend! Be set aglow with the fire of the love of God, so that the hearts of the people will become enlightened by the light of thy love.
>
> Supplicate to God, pray to Him and invoke Him at midnight and at dawn. Be humble and submissive to God and chant the verses of thanksgiving at morn and eve, for that He guided thee unto the Manifest Light and showed to thee the straight Path and destined to thee the station of nearness in His wonderful Kingdom. Verily I ask God to augment for thee, every day, the light of guidance and His gift of virtue, comfort and ease.[166]
>
> *'Abdu'l-Bahá*

To spread light in darkness, openness in closed minds, peace where there is war, is essentially what we as Bahá'ís are engaged in doing. Our vision, given to us by Bahá'u'lláh, is a united and peaceful world. Love is the foundation for this peace. Let us therefore become the tools of love, peace and enlightenment.

> Love is greater than peace, for peace is founded upon love. Love is the objective point of peace, and peace is an outcome of love.

Until love is attained, peace cannot be; but there is a so-called peace without love. The love which is from God is the fundamental. This love is the object of all human attainment, the radiance of heaven, the light of man.[167]

'Abdu'l-Bahá

The portals of His blessings are opened wide and His signs are published abroad and the glory of truth is blazing forth; inexhaustible are the blessings. Know ye the value of this time. Strive ye with all your hearts, raise up your voices and shout, until this dark world be filled with light, and this narrow place of shadows be widened out, and this dust heap of a fleeting moment be changed into a mirror for the eternal gardens of heaven, and this globe of earth receive its portion of celestial grace.

Then will aggression crumble away, and all that maketh for disunity be destroyed, and the structure of oneness be raised – that the Blessed Tree may cast its shade over east and west, and the Tabernacle of the singleness of man be set up on the high summits, and flags that betoken love and fellowship flutter from their staffs around the world until the sea of truth lift high its waves, and earth bring forth the roses and sweet herbs of blessings without end, and become from pole to pole the Abhá Paradise.[168]

'Abdu'l-Bahá

PART III

WALKING THE PATH OF DIVINE LOVE: SOME SUGGESTIONS FOR SPIRITUAL EXERCISES

The practice of divine love requires of us a perspective rather different from our usual outlook. The suggestions for spiritual exercises formulated here aim at changing your ordinary frame of mind into one in which divine love becomes a predominant perspective on everything you do.

Love is always a relationship: between you and God, between you and other human beings. Divine love, being essentially unconditioned by any created thing and any human relation, can be developed in the relationship between you and God represented by His Manifestation for this age, Bahá'u'lláh, or by His Exemplar, 'Abdu'l-Bahá. While it is essential for each one of us to relate to these sources of eternal spiritual love and light if we are to experience the power of divine love and become confirmed in our belief in an eternal, transcendent reality, we must be careful not to obstruct the outpourings of God's endless love by trying to keep it for ourselves. We must rather endeavour to let the living waters of love pass through us by constantly pouring it out to others through our attitudes, our words and our deeds. This will reinforce our connection with the endless ocean of mercy, which in return will pour ever more of its joy-creating, energizing and vitalizing energies into our lives.

The following exercises are of course no complete guide into this vast arena. They aim at two achievements: to create a spiritual condition in which each individual becomes receptive to the experience of the presence of the divine spirit of love in his own heart and mind, and, secondly, to change our attitude towards others and the world so that we will perceive our fellow human beings in the light of true unity. The exercises do not prescribe a specific code of behaviour – the Bahá'í writings abound in good suggestions in this respect and we are supposed to study them every morning and evening. They rather aim at initiating a process by which the guidance from the writings may be internalized in each of us so that we, inspired by the utterances of the Sacred Writings and confirmed by the Holy Spirit, may enter into a creative process to revitalize our own lives and all our human relationships and be entirely submerged in the sea of love and service. The focus of these exercises, then, is to enhance our ability to become channels for this power by enabling us to uncover and experience the joy of divine love present in our own hearts and in our human relationships.

One main focus of this training programme is learning to exploit the principle of the Holy Spirit in order to be able to practise divine love. This principle, which is explained more extensively earlier in this book, defines how we can obtain assistance in situations where we are powerless, or do not know; it consists in acknowledging our weakness and calling upon the assistance of divine power. In this context, we should always bear in mind that the first emanation of the Holy Spirit is the inspiration that the Manifestation of God receives, leading Him to formulate this inspiration in His Writings. We should therefore always look to the Writings of Bahá'u'lláh, as well as to those of 'Abdu'l-Bahá, the Centre of His Covenant, of the Guardian, and the institutions of the Faith, to find the basic principles that will best guide society and our individual lives. We must never misuse what we may construe as our own inspiration and guidance to question the truth and validity of what is set down in the Bahá'í writings. The guidance given individually to every single member of humanity by the inspiration of the Holy Spirit is intended to assist us in finding the specific ways and means of fulfilling the ordinances and exhortations formulated in the writings. The validity of this individual guidance offered by the Holy Spirit is in the Dispensation of Bahá'u'lláh confined to the single individual who receives it. We should not impose it on others, nor even talk too much about it. Ideas and thoughts received by individuals may provide valuable insight, even to consulting bodies in the administration, but is then subject to the decisions taken.

Implicit in the Bahá'í writings is the promise that divine assistance will support any effort which is concordant with the purposes and tasks formulated in the Covenant. Certainly, developing love and unity, sharing the transcendent happiness immanent in these with others, and serving the world of humanity are entirely consistent with the Covenant, and as long as this is your intention you can feel entirely assured that the Holy Spirit will help and guide you in your efforts.

Please remember that the following procedures are only personal suggestions, and as such without any authority in the writings. You should *not* teach these procedures to non-Bahá'ís as though they were an integral part of the Bahá'í Faith. You should never think that these exercises are a prerequisite for spiritual growth for everyone, as the requisites for this are clearly stated in the writings themselves. The exercises are for your personal use, and the right places to discuss them are seminars and institutes where Bahá'ís who are particularly interested in prayer and meditation look for more detailed and specific approaches, and are spontaneously and joyfully motivated to impose on themselves a greater discipline in these matters for a *limited period* in their lives. Of course you may share them with others who express this particular longing and interest. The main point is that there are many ways to come in touch with divine love, and the suggestions presented here are not the only ones. Of course, you will use these procedures yourself only if you feel comfortable with them, and think that you can profit by using them.

While carrying out these exercises it is supposed that you are fulfilling the minimum requirements of Bahá'u'lláh's Covenant with respect to daily prayer and meditation: reciting the holy verses every morning and evening, saying your obligatory prayer, and repeating the Greatest Name ("Alláh-u-Abhá") 95 times each day. In relation to the last of these, let us begin with Exercise 1.

EXERCISE 1
REMEMBRANCE OF GOD

The first exercise is focused on the use of the Greatest Name. The recital of the Greatest Name, "Alláh-u-Abhá", 95 times each day is one of the laws of the Kitáb-i-Aqdas. Bahá'u'lláh reveals:

> It hath been ordained that every believer in God, the Lord of Judgement, shall, each day, having washed his hands and then his face, seat himself and, turning unto God, repeat "Alláh-u-Abhá" ninety-five times. Such was the decree of the Maker of the Heavens when, with majesty and power, He established Himself upon the thrones of His Names.[169]

This meditation can be seen as a way of training your ability to turn entirely to God and to forget everything but Him. Although this meditation is not the only way to achieve this ability, it is one that is strongly recommended by Bahá'u'lláh Himself and is binding on all believers. Here are some suggestions for how the meditation on the Greatest Name can be carried out (for a more detailed exposition, see my earlier book, *Unlocking the Gate of the Heart*, pp. 149–66).

Repetitions

The Greatest Name is to be repeated 95 times (= 5 x 19) in one session each day. There are many ways of keeping count, but perhaps one of the easiest ways is to use a rosary or prayer beads with 95 separate beads. The rosary should have a stopper so that the hand will feel when 95 repetitions are done. If the beads are large, they can be pulled over the middle joint of the index finger with the thumb. If the beads are smaller, one can use the middle finger to pull them from between the thumb and ring fingers, which are held together tip to tip.

Meditation on the Greatest Name thus requires the combining of a physical activity (the counting process) with a mental or spiritual activity. It is only sensible to suggest that awareness is primarily focused on the Greatest Name, not on the counting of the fingers.

Posture

Bahá'u'lláh specifies that one should be seated while performing this meditation. It is not necessary to face the Qiblih, although you may wish to do so.

Recitation

The Greatest Name may be recited either aloud or silently within yourself. The writings do not seem to emphasize one way or the other. The word "recitation" is often applied to this type of meditation, as well as for the reading of Bahá'u'lláh's Writings. This word suggests more of a singing tone than one of speaking. Try to "sing" the word in one single tone. This makes the syllables of the word ring more clearly.

Eyes can be kept open or closed (no particular suggestion on this is found in the writings). If you choose to keep your eyes open, avoid using them actively. Instead, try to focus them on one point, or keep them unfocused. Your attention should primarily be focused on the sound of the word, and on the spiritual content of the name, not on what you see with your open eyes.

Suggestions for beginners

Generally a meditation that is carried out silently (without using the voice), and with closed eyes, will be of greater benefit in the development of "inner hearing" and "inner sight". This can be important for someone who is just beginning to meditate.

Nevertheless, those who have the tendency to daydream or lose themselves in other thoughts may find it easier to say the Greatest Name aloud, or with their eyes open.

One suggestion is to start by saying the Greatest Name aloud, and eventually begin to say it more and more quietly. Then start saying the Greatest Name mentally, just by thinking the sound of the words. Finally, just listen for the Greatest Name ringing in your consciousness without any effort on your part.

Flexibility

You may spontaneously want to change the way you are intoning the Greatest Name: faster or slower, stronger or weaker, higher or lower. Remain susceptible to such impulses – let it happen. If the tempo changes, the physical part of the activity (the counting) must also change in synchronization. Let the Name decide the tempo, not your fingers.

Ablutions

This meditation should be preceded by ablutions, i.e. washing hands and face.

Forgetting all save God and calling upon His spirit

Meditation on the Greatest Name is an aid to forgetting all save God and calling upon His spirit. Two aspects of this can be discerned: one is in putting aside the thoughts and worries which take hold of the mind and hinder the awareness from completely turning towards God. The other is in turning the inner senses towards the countenance of God and invoking His power. These two aspects, which we will discuss separately, are actually inter-dependent. If we are to receive inspiration from God, our mind must be emptied and purified, our heart entirely directed towards God, as 'Abdu'l-Bahá explains:

> I now assure thee, O servant of God, that if thy mind become empty and pure from every mention and thought and thy heart

attracted wholly to the Kingdom of God, forget all else besides God and come in communion with the Spirit of God, then the Holy Spirit will assist thee with a power which will enable thee to penetrate all things, and a Dazzling Spark which enlightens all sides, a Brilliant Flame in the zenith of the heavens, will teach thee that which thou dost not know of the facts of the universe and of the divine doctrine.[170]

'Abdu'l-Bahá

Here are some suggestions on how to carry this out in practice:

Calming the mind

While you are mentally repeating the Greatest Name, try to listen to how its sound resonates in your mind. If your thoughts wander, calmly refocus upon the Greatest Name. Thoughts have a sound in your mind. Practise letting go of thoughts by refocusing your awareness from listening to the sound of your thoughts to the sound of the Greatest Name. This refocusing should be gentle and gradual, without effort to force thoughts away. When you actively reject thoughts during meditation, it can lead to the unhealthy habit of suppressing your own thoughts. This can result in these thoughts returning with greater force in the long run. Rather, let your thoughts flow freely as you gently set the sound of the Greatest Name at the centre of your awareness once again.

Invocation

When you have reached a relaxed, aware and thought-less state while using the Greatest Name, try directing your awareness towards God. Use the Greatest Name to call upon the Spirit of God. Even though the call (or invocation) goes out from you towards the heavenly realm, you remain earthly and humbly open. Keep the sound of the Name close to you. Maintain a calm, non-judgemental, and open attitude while you repeat the Greatest Name. Use its sound to gently give any of your thoughts less attention. Through the process of invocation, we approach the Holy Presence.

O Son of Light! Forget all save Me and commune with My spirit. This is of the essence of My command, therefore turn unto it.[171]

Bahá'u'lláh

O Son of Being! Thy heart is My home; sanctify it for My descent. Thy spirit is My place of revelation; cleanse it for My manifestation.[172]

Bahá'u'lláh

EXERCISE 2
"IGNITE . . . WITHIN MY BREAST THE FIRE OF THY LOVE . . ."

Unlock, O people, the gates of the hearts of men with the keys of the remembrance of Him Who is the Remembrance of God and the Source of wisdom amongst you. He hath chosen out of the whole world the hearts of His servants, and made them each a seat for the revelation of His glory. Wherefore, sanctify them from every defilement, that the things for which they were created may be engraven upon them. This indeed is a token of God's bountiful favour . . .

Strive, O people, that your eyes may be directed towards the mercy of God, that your hearts may be attuned to His wondrous remembrance, that your souls may rest confidently upon His grace and bounty, that your feet may tread the path of His good-pleasure.[173]

Bahá'u'lláh

For love of God and spiritual attraction do cleanse and purify the human heart and dress and adorn it with the spotless garment of holiness; and once the heart is entirely attached to the Lord, and bound over to the Blessed Perfection, then will the grace of God be revealed.

This love is not of the body but completely of the soul. And those souls whose inner being is lit by the love of God are even as spreading rays of light, and they shine out like stars of holiness in a pure and crystalline sky . . .

. . . Let them behold the Blessed Beauty, and feel the flame and rapture of that meeting, and be struck dumb with awe and wonder.[174]

'Abdu'l-Bahá

If you find you need to visualize someone when you pray, think of the Master. Through Him you can address Bahá'u'lláh. Gradually try to think of the qualities of the Manifestation, and in that way a mental form will fade out, for after all the body is not the thing, His Spirit is there and is the essential, everlasting element.[175]

Written on behalf of Shoghi Effendi

The following exercises should be carried out daily (five to ten minutes) for a few days or weeks, before you go on in this programme. The above quotations define the objective of the meditation, and suggest a method to attain it.

In this meditation, your physical heart, or chest, will be used as a symbol of your spiritual heart, i.e. the centre of your entire being, your self. The purpose of this exercise is to develop love and devotion towards the Centre of the Covenant, 'Abdu'l-Bahá, and through this, to be able to focus the heart entirely on God's love.

- Read stories about the life of 'Abdu'l-Bahá, or read His Writings. Study a picture of 'Abdu'l-Bahá. Then close your eyes and centre your attention in your chest.

- Picture what you have just read or seen with your inner eye, while letting your love for God, Bahá'u'lláh or 'Abdu'l-Bahá glow in your chest.

- Let the mental image eventually disappear, while keeping your heart turned towards the spiritual centre of love, light, and power.

- Learn the following prayer by heart, and use it before beginning the meditation:

Ignite, then, O my God, within my breast the fire of Thy love, that its flame may burn up all else except my remembrance of Thee, that every trace of corrupt desire may be entirely mortified within me, and that naught may remain except the glorification of Thy transcendent and all-glorious Being. This is my highest aspiration, mine ardent desire, O Thou Who rulest all things, and in Whose hand is the kingdom of the entire creation. Thou, verily, doest what Thou choosest. No God is there beside Thee, the Almighty, the All-Glorious, the Ever-Forgiving.[176]

Bahá'u'lláh

O Son of Man! Rejoice in the gladness of thine heart, that thou mayest be worthy to meet Me and to mirror forth My beauty.[177]

Bahá'u'lláh

* * *

The two previous exercises will be useful as parts of the following ones. The latter, however, are not cumulative, but should each be carried out one by one over a limited period of time.

On each of them you should spend a few days to a maximum of a couple of weeks. When you have gone through all of them, you can review them, going through them once more. If you work intensively with them for a limited period of time, you will probably experience that they will change your life in some respect, and increase your joy and radiance.

Having put them aside for a while, return to them after a few months if you find that you are slipping back into old mental habits. The goal of the exercises is that the spiritual perspective they induce shall be a permanent and integrated part of the way you look at the world, and a natural way of relating to your fellow human beings. The exercises are helpful in taking this step, but unlike the obligatory prayers and other fundamental spiritual exercises they are not designed to preoccupy you for the rest of your life.

EXERCISE 3
I CHOOSE TO SEE THE WORLD IN THE LIGHT OF DIVINE LOVE

O Man of Two Visions! Close one eye and open the other. Close one to the world and all that is therein, and open the other to the hallowed beauty of the Beloved.[178]

Bahá'u'lláh

Upon the inmost reality of each and every created thing He hath shed the light of one of His names, and made it a recipient of the glory of one of His attributes. Upon the reality of man, however, He hath focused the radiance of all of His names and attributes, and made it a mirror of His own Self.[179]

Bahá'u'lláh

He hath chosen out of the whole world the hearts of His servants, and made them each a seat for the revelation of His glory. Wherefore, sanctify them from every defilement, that the things for which they were created may be engraven upon them.[180]

Bahá'u'lláh

Suggestion for meditation every morning and evening (approximately 15 minutes):

1. Read through the quotations above. Learn by heart the Hidden Word (the first quotation). Repeat it every time you begin this meditation.

2. Pray to God to assist and guide you to realize the meaning of the Word.

3. Look around you in the room or place where you are. Do not select any particular thing which may be beautiful or attractive, do not avoid seeing anything which may be repulsive or ugly.

4. Everything you see can be seen with the eye of your ego, your lower self. Your ego harbours feelings such as desire, hatred, depression, fear, anxiety, disgust or indifference. As you look at each thing, say to yourself:

   "I can see that _____(substitute name of thing) *as an object of my*_____ *"* (substitute a word such as one of those mentioned above).

   Be sure not to dwell long on any feeling. If you discover that you are caught up in your thoughts and feelings, gently correct yourself by looking at other objects, and observe these in the same way. The point is for you to be able to witness some of the habits of your lower self, not to indulge in them.

5. Close your eyes. With your inner eye, see the room you just saw. Now as you look at each thing with eyes closed, repeat the same sentence:

   "I can see that _____(substitute name of thing) *as an object of my*_____ *"* (substitute the word such as mentioned above).

6. Now tell yourself: *"This is the world my ego has created. But I can decide to see the world as God created it."* Now use the Greatest Name as an invocation (Yá Bahá'u'l-Abhá!), and for a short while try not to think of anything. No image, no thought, no noise of words lingering in your mind, only silence and awareness for a few seconds: thus you try to forget everything but God.

7. Now open your eyes, look around you at things without being selective, and tell each thing:

"I see in you_____" (an attribute of God, such as beauty, grandeur, knowledge, cohesion, unity, love, light, strength, power, variety, creativity, ingenuity, craftmanship, perfection, joy, etc.).

8. Close your eyes again, look at the room with closed eyes, and tell each thing:

"I see in you_____" (an attribute of God, such as beauty, grandeur, knowledge, cohesion, unity, love, light, strength, power, variety, creativity, ingenuity, craftmanship, perfection, joy, etc.).

9. To end, use the Greatest Name as an invocation again, make your heart pure and holy by dropping all thoughts, all images, and rest for a little while in the peace, happiness and joy created by seeing the world as God intended it, centred in your heart which is the home of God. Or, if you prefer, carry out the meditation on the Greatest Name, repeating it 95 times.

10. Open your eyes, resolve to try to see the world in this light as often as you can today, telling each thing silently that it is God's blessed creation, that every thing is a door to His knowledge, reflecting His Names.

11. Having said the midday prayer, sit down for two minutes, close your eyes, and think about how this exercise may help you fulfil your purpose to know and worship God.

Reflect also upon the helplessness and poverty of your ego's thoughts, and the richness and strength of God's way of looking at the world, a way of looking that you can share.

EXERCISE 4
I REGARD MYSELF IN THE SAME WAY AS GOD REGARDS ME

O Son of Spirit! I created thee rich, why dost thou bring thyself down to poverty? Noble I made thee, wherewith dost thou abase thyself? Out of the essence of knowledge I gave thee being, why seekest thou enlightenment from anyone beside Me? Out of the clay of love I moulded thee, how dost thou busy thyself with another? Turn thy sight unto thyself, that thou mayest find Me standing within thee, mighty, powerful and self-subsisting.[181]

Bahá'u'lláh

O Son of Being! With the hands of power I made thee and with the fingers of strength I created thee; and within thee have I placed the essence of My light. Be thou content with it and seek naught else, for My work is perfect and My command is binding. Question it not, nor have a doubt thereof.[182]

Bahá'u'lláh

O Son of Man! Thou art My dominion and My dominion perisheth not; wherefore fearest thou thy perishing? Thou art My light and My light shall never be extinguished; why dost thou dread extinction? Thou art My glory and My glory fadeth not; thou art My robe and My robe shall never be outworn. Abide then in thy love for Me, that thou mayest find Me in the realm of glory.[183]

Bahá'u'lláh

O Son of Being! Thou art My lamp and My light is in thee. Get thou from it thy radiance and seek none other than Me. For I have created thee rich and have bountifully shed My favour upon thee.[184]

Bahá'u'lláh

O Son of Being! My love is My stronghold; he that entereth therein is safe and secure, and he that turneth away shall surely stray and perish.[185]

Bahá'u'lláh

O Son of Utterance! Thou art My stronghold; enter therein that thou mayest abide in safety. My love is in thee, know it, that thou mayest find Me near unto thee.[186]

Bahá'u'lláh

Suggestions for meditation every morning and evening (approximately 15 minutes):

1. Choose one of the Hidden Words above for one exercise. Learn it by heart, apply the procedure below in meditation upon it a few days. Then choose another one, go through the same procedure. Thus, you may spend one to three weeks with this exercise.

2. Start the meditation by repeating the Hidden Word you have selected. Pray for God's assistance to understand it and to experience its reality in your own life.

3. Now formulate a response to the Hidden Word in the form of a short, positive affirmation of the type:

"I believe that this is my true identity."

"I will believe what God says I am, rather than what other people think I am."

"I am willing to change my ideas about what I am, to conform with what Bahá'u'lláh says I am, as He knows better."

"In my heart I find _____" (select one attribute from the quotation, such as nobility, love, light, strength, glory, eternal life).

"My shortcomings are unimportant and do not last, but my eternal qualities are everlasting."

"I will seek the safety of God's love in the depth of my own heart."

"Nothing that happens to me in this world can ever take away from me the eternal quality of _____" (select a quality).

"When I stay with the Love of God, I am perfectly and eternally safe."

"If this is true, nothing and no one in this world can ever really hurt me."

You can find your own formulation, your own way of responding to God's statement about you.

4. Having formulated an affirmation about your true identity, pray that the Holy Spirit will teach you about your true self. Close your eyes, invoke the Holy Spirit by using the Greatest Name (Yá Bahá'u'l-Abhá!), forget every thought and idea in your mind for a moment, and enjoy silence for a short while.

5. Repeat your affirmation; now ask how this can be true for your own life. Then listen to the thoughts that come to your mind. In order to start this new kind of thinking, which is the thinking of your higher self, it can be helpful to try to imagine that 'Abdu'l-Bahá is speaking to you about the subject. It is the wisdom of God deposited in your own soul that you now listen to. The thoughts given you by the Holy Spirit are always loving, they are full of assurance, and they give peace to your heart. Listen in silence to what your higher self can tell you about your true and eternal identity.

6. If disturbing thoughts enter, do not become annoyed or distressed, but quietly repeat your affirmation and ask for more guidance about your true identity.

7. Sink into the quietness and peace of your own heart for a while. If you prefer, carry out the meditation on the Greatest Name, repeating it 95 times.

8. Open your eyes, be determined to remember your affirmation throughout the day.

9. Throughout the day, remind yourself often of your true identity by repeating your affirmation.

10. After having said the midday prayer, sit down for a couple of minutes. Bear witness there and then to your poverty with regard to understanding your own identity apart from what God teaches you about yourself. Think about how God's strength can become the source of your strength, and how the strength that is the product of your own ego is in fact your own weakness. Think about what true humility is: is it to accept what God tells you, or to insist on your own concepts?

EXERCISE 5
I WILL LIVE THE DAYS OF MY LIFE WITH MY MIND STAINLESS, MY HEART UNSULLIED

O Son of Earth! Wouldst thou have Me, seek none other than Me; and wouldst thou gaze upon My beauty, close thine eyes to the world and all that is therein; for My will and the will of another than Me, even as fire and water, cannot dwell together in one heart.[187]

Bahá'u'lláh

O Companion of My Throne! Hear no evil, and see no evil, abase not thyself, neither sigh and weep. Speak no evil, that thou mayest not hear it spoken unto thee, and magnify not the faults of others that thine own faults may not appear great; and wish not the abasement of anyone, that thine own abasement be not exposed. Live then the days of thy life, that are less than a fleeting moment, with thy mind stainless, thy heart unsullied, thy thoughts pure, and thy nature sanctified, so that, free and content, thou mayest put away this mortal frame, and repair unto the mystic paradise and abide in the eternal kingdom for evermore.[188]

Bahá'u'lláh

They whose hearts are warmed by the energizing influence of God's creative love cherish His creatures for His sake, and recognize in every human face a sign of His reflected glory.[189]

Shoghi Effendi

Suggestions for meditation every morning and evening, 15 minutes each time:

1. Read and learn by heart one of the Hidden Words above.

2. Read the first Hidden Word again. Formulate a short affirmation, in which you state your willingness to let go of "the world", i.e. everything but God's will. For example: "I will seek none other than Thee."

   "Let Thy will be my will."

   "I let go of everything that is not of Thee."

3. Wash your hands and face, as a symbol that you are purifying yourself from everything but God.

4. Now read the the second Hidden Word, and consider that whenever you become busy with the weaknesses of others, their mistakes, their bad sides, you are letting veils come between you and God's realm of mercy. Your grievances may be your strongest attachments to the world. You must make a choice: If you choose to keep your bitterness, your annoyance, your feeling of being hurt and victimized by others, you will lose the purity of heart that brings you closer to God. God wills love and unity for you, and another will is incompatible with His will. Either you let your enemies go, or you lose Him. Repeat your affirmation to cling to His will.

5. Think of different people who have hurt you, people who have made you angry, spoilt your life, disappointed you, people you prefer not to meet – in short, those whose weaknesses have been indeed felt by you. To the extent that you go on harbouring bad feelings about them, you close yourself out from heaven. The quality of divine love is such as to encompass everyone, without exception.

6. Closing your eyes, use the Greatest Name as invocation, seek His mercy for a short while, forgetting everything else; implore

His help to assist you to see these persons in another way, the way God created them. He certainly created everyone good and with a pure heart.

7. Now visualize those towards whom you bear some sort of grudge. Tell him or her in your mind how God looks at him, how much He loves him, which divine qualities He endowed his soul with. If this is difficult, imagine 'Abdu'l-Bahá standing at your side and listen to how He would formulate it. Remember that the face of your fellow human being, whom you do not especially like, is God's face. Try to see each one surrounded by the light of God's love. As you do so, your own heart is released from the prison of the ego, and you are approaching the mystic paradise, the ancient sovereignty bequeathed to the pure heart.

8. At last, pray for everyone, and while you pray, envelop everyone in the light of God's love, and be thankful that by the aid of these people whom you formerly considered your enemies, you have now been able to come closer to God.

9. After having said the short midday prayer, ponder the true meaning of the words: "There is none other God but Thee". God, as revealed through His Manifestation for this day, wishes your heart to be entirely reserved for Him. Can you let go of all other gods, who are nothing but illusions made up by your own mind, separating you from Him?

10. Throughout the day, repeat your affirmation often (the one you made under no. 2), and whoever you meet or see, tell him in your mind: "God created you out of His love. I look at the purity and innocence of your soul as God created it. I will love you with the love that God cast into my heart."

11. Having practised these ten points for a few days, you might like to expand your realization of the oneness of mankind by reflecting on these words as well:

Love the creatures for the sake of God and not for themselves. You will never become angry or impatient if you love them for the sake of God. Humanity is not perfect. There are imperfections in every human being, and you will always become unhappy if you look toward the people themselves. But if you look toward God, you will love them and be kind to them, for the world of God is the world of perfection and complete mercy. Therefore, do not look at the shortcomings of anybody; see with the sight of forgiveness. The imperfect eye beholds imperfections. The eye that covers faults looks toward the Creator of souls. He created them, trains and provides for them, endows them with capacity and life, sight and hearing; therefore, they are the signs of His grandeur.[190]

'Abdu'l-Bahá

One must see in every human being only that which is worthy of praise. When this is done, one can be a friend to the whole human race. If, however, we look at people from the standpoint of their faults, then being a friend to them is a formidable task.[191]

'Abdu'l-Bahá

O ye lovers of this wronged one! Cleanse ye your eyes, so that ye behold no man as different from yourselves. See ye no strangers; rather see all men as friends, for love and unity come hard when ye fix your gaze on otherness. And in this new and wondrous age, the Holy Writings say that we must be at one with every people; that we must see neither harshness nor injustice, neither malevolence, nor hostility, nor hate, but rather turn our eyes toward the heaven of ancient glory. For each of the creatures is a sign of God, and it was by the grace of the Lord and His power that each did step into the world; therefore they are not strangers, but in the family; not aliens, but friends, and to be treated as such.[192]

'Abdu'l-Bahá

The love which exists between the hearts of believers is prompted by the ideal of the unity of spirits. This love is attained through the knowledge of God, so that men see the Divine Love reflected in the heart. Each sees in the other the Beauty of God reflected in the soul, and finding this point of similarity, they are attracted to one another in love. This love will make all men the waves of one sea, this love will make them all the stars of one heaven and the fruits of one tree. This love will bring the realization of true accord, the foundation of real unity.[193]

'Abdu'l-Bahá

EXERCISE 6
I WILL REGARD CALAMITIES AS GOD'S MERCY

O Son of Man! My calamity is My providence, outwardly it is fire and vengeance, but inwardly it is light and mercy. Hasten thereunto that thou mayest become an eternal light and an immortal spirit. This is My command unto thee, do thou observe it.[194]

Bahá'u'lláh

O Son of Man! For everything there is a sign. The sign of love is fortitude under My decree and patience under My trials.[195]

Bahá'u'lláh

O Son of Man! The true lover yearneth for tribulation even as doth the rebel for forgiveness and the sinful for mercy.[196]

Bahá'u'lláh

. . . all the sorrow and the grief that exist come from the world of matter – the spiritual world bestows only the joy!

If we suffer, it is the outcome of material things, and all the trials and troubles come from this world of illusion.[197]

'Abdu'l-Bahá

For every one of you his paramount duty is to choose for himself that on which no other may infringe and none usurp from him. Such a thing – and to this the Almighty is My witness – is the love of God, could ye but perceive it.

Build ye for yourselves such houses as the rain and floods can never destroy, which shall protect you from the changes and chances of this life. This is the instruction of Him Whom the world hath wronged and forsaken.[198]

Bahá'u'lláh

Suggestions for meditation:

1. Study the quotations above.

2. Consider that suffering comes from the material world. It pertains to your body. Attachment to the world of matter necessarily creates pain, as everything in this world is perishable and you will inevitably lose whatever object you are clinging to. Only the love of God can ensure you eternal happiness, because it is eternal, and because love is inherently happiness.

3. Some of the most burning questions in human life concern suffering and tribulation. Consider the quotations above, then ask the Holy Spirit, your higher self, to explain for you anything that seems unclear to you in this respect. Close your eyes, invoke the Greatest Name and listen to your wise thoughts on this subject, wise thoughts that are undisturbed by all the tribulations and noise of this world.

4. Realize that since the Holy Spirit guides you in this matter, it will guide you and protect you always and in eternity. You are not essentially a body, but an eternal soul entitled to eternal happiness and love.

5. Man is body and soul, and between these inner and outer realities there is an intermediary faculty. This exercise makes use of this faculty by means of breathing.

    With the assurance that you are not only a body, sit down, close your eyes, turn your attention to your body, first of all your breath. While you breathe, observe your breathing. If you take a long breath, tell yourself: I am taking a long breath. If you take a short breath, tell yourself: I am taking a short breath, etc. If your attention wanders, gently correct yourself.

6. Now direct your attention towards the different parts of your body and bear witness before God to the feelings you find. Do not go into the feelings and merge with them, but pay

attention to them for a short period of time, and tell yourself before God, or before 'Abdu'l-Bahá, such things as:

"I am feeling sadness."

"I am feeling pain."

"I am feeling powerless."

"I am feeling anger."

"I am feeling desire."

"I am feeling pride."

"I am feeling joy."

"I feel nothing at all."

7. (Optional). Love is also acceptance. Therefore, accepting your feelings means developing your love. Feelings of pain and sorrow can be hard to accept, and if you think you need to give particular attention to this, you can try the following procedure:

Breathe deeply in and out with your stomach. Make the exhalations lengthy, almost like a sigh, and as you exhale direct your attention to your own body; feel the pain, and say to yourself: I accept this. Now breathe deeply in, feel how the breath fills your whole body with life and light. As you are doing this, direct your inner gaze outward towards God's light, towards His aid and mercy, filling yourself with it as you inhale, praying a short prayer: "Help me, fill me with your strength." Breathe like this for a few minutes. In this way, you are using your breath to declare your own powerlessness and poverty and God's strength and wealth.

8. Having borne witness to your weakness for a few minutes, turn to God, invoke His Name, and ask Him to envelop and

submerge you in His love, His strength, His care. Remember that love is happiness. Try to find it in yourself.

At this point you may carry out the meditation on the Greatest Name, and reinforce it through breathing in synchronization with the Word (see *Unlocking the Gate of the Heart*, Appendix 3).

9. Today, whenever you are not too busy, remember to breathe consciously and often invoke the Greatest Name ("Yá Bahá'u'l-Abhá") silently. When you walk, be aware that you are walking, when you eat, be aware that you are eating, thus exercise composure in all situations.

10. When saying the midday prayer, reflect on the fact that your weakness and poverty is the state your body is in, whereas God's strength is available for you to help sustain your life and deal with your challenges. He is truly "the Help in Peril, the Self-Subsisting", meaning, among other things: He rests in Himself, unaffected by the changes and chances of this world, and at the same time is extending His help and assistance to you. Seek this assistance today!

EXERCISE 7
I LOOK TOWARDS GOD IN ALL SITUATIONS

He ['Abdu'l-Bahá] was asked "How shall I overcome seeing the faults of others – recognizing the wrong in others?", and He replied: "I will tell you. Whenever you recognize the fault of another, think of yourself! What are my imperfections? – and try to remove them. Do this whenever you are tried through the words or deeds of others. Thus you will grow, become more perfect. You will overcome self, you will not even have time to think of the faults of others . . ."[199]

'Abdu'l-Bahá

If any differences arise amongst you, behold Me standing before your face, and overlook the faults of one another for My name's sake and as a token of your love for My manifest and resplendent Cause.[200]

Bahá'u'lláh

Trust in God, and be unmoved by either the praise or the false accusations . . . depend entirely on God.[201]

'Abdu'l-Bahá

We fain would hope that the people of Bahá may be guided by the blessed words: "Say: all things are of God." This exalted utterance is like unto water for quenching the fire of hate and enmity which smouldereth within the hearts and breasts of men. By this single utterance contending peoples and kindreds will attain the light of true unity. Verily He speaketh the truth and leadeth the way. He is the All-Powerful, the Exalted, the Gracious.[202]

Bahá'u'lláh

Armed with the power of Thy love, the hatred which moveth them that are against Thee can never alarm me; and with Thy praise on my lips, the rulings of Thy decree can in no wise fill me with sorrow.[203]

Bahá'u'lláh

These quotations show us different ways of relating to other people in difficult situations.

1. Every morning and evening study the quotations above.

2. In an acute situation of conflict with others, try the following:

   (1) Be aware of your own emotions and feelings. Accept that your primary duty is to deal adequately with them (compare the first quotation).

   (2) In conflict situations our lower, animal self has three strategies, which all aim at protecting your physical self: *attack, flight, or compliance* (i.e. being superficially kind, pretending subordination). These reactions occur in different representations among the ideas in your ego's thought system. Belief in these ideas will limit you with regard to practising true love, which comes from your higher self.

Such false beliefs could be:

• *related to the attack mode of your ego*:
"I can gain what I want if I manage to control others through my rage, my anger, my blame, or having them feel guilt by crying and weeping."

"I have the power to change another person's behaviour."

• *related to the flight mode of your ego:*
"I can avoid problems by becoming indifferent. It's better to shut down and withdraw than to reach out and risk rejection."

"I am not good enough, so I have to . . ."

• *related to the compliant mode of your ego:*
"If I do things to make myself happy, I'm selfish. In order to be unselfish, I have to sacrifice myself and make others happy, otherwise they will not love me."

"What I feel and want is not important."

"I should never do anything that might upset others."

3. Spend some time identifying which of the three strategies your ego prefers to use in different situations and with different people. Learning to know the strategies of your ego will help you fulfil the words of 'Abdu'l-Bahá when you are in a critical situation. He suggests that when you constantly have the intention to learn and improve, you will overcome self and not have the time and attention to dwell on the mistakes of others.

4. If a conflict situation occurs, you must immediately turn your attention to yourself. Ask yourself: "What strategy am I now inclined to use?" (attack, flight or compliance). Name it, and in doing so, witness your own powerlessness to deal with the situation adequately, as all these options for behaviour are suggested to you by your lower self.

5. Being aware that you are powerless, call on God's strength and assistance; surely the Holy Spirit is omnipresent and will help you. Remember Bahá'u'lláh's words: "Behold Me standing before your face." Invoke the Greatest Name, and be sure to direct yourself towards the presence of His spirit, confident that His wisdom and love are there, available for you.

6. Ask then for His guidance as to what to do and say; pray for His assistance. Consider now the problem at hand, thinking of Bahá'u'lláh's words: "all things are of God . . ." Courage is necessary to practise love, and courage means taking the risk

of pain, as opposed to self-protection. Listen to the thoughts that come to you from your higher self.

Love is a light that never dwelleth in a heart possessed by fear . . .

A lover feareth nothing and no harm can come nigh him . . .

The steed of this Valley [of love] is pain . . .

. . . at every step he throweth a thousand heads at the feet of the Beloved.[204]

Bahá'u'lláh

7. Afterwards, when you are out of the situation, evaluate how you managed to act. Be patient with yourself, be sure God is forgiving and loving with regard to your shortcomings. Determine what you want to give attention to next time you are in a difficult situation.

Finish your evaluation by rehearsing this sequence of mental operations you are to perform in a critical situation:

- Be aware of your own reactions. Observe them sufficiently to know what your preferred strategy would be, and name it.

- Then acknowledge your weakness, call on the presence of God, listen to His wisdom, considering that all things are of God.

- Be courageous, i.e. risk a passing pain rather than protecting yourself.

8. In your midday prayer you bear witness to the powerlessness of your ego's strategies, and affirm your belief that God will guide you, through His strength.

9. The following prayer and meditation can reinforce your ability to deal with difficult situations adequately:

145

Glorified art Thou, O my God! I yield Thee thanks that Thou hast made known unto me Him Who is the Day-Spring of Thy mercy, and the Dawning-Place of Thy grace, and the Repository of Thy Cause. I beseech Thee by Thy Name, through which the faces of them that are nigh unto Thee have turned white, and the hearts of such as are devoted to Thee have winged their flight towards Thee, to grant that I may, at all times and under all conditions, lay hold on Thy cord, and be rid of all attachment to anyone except Thee, and may keep mine eyes directed towards the horizon of Thy Revelation, and may carry out what Thou hast prescribed unto me in Thy Tablets.

Attire, O my Lord, both my inner and outer being with the raiment of Thy favours and Thy loving-kindness. Keep me safe, then, from whatsoever may be abhorrent unto Thee, and graciously assist me and my kindred to obey Thee, and to shun whatsoever may stir up any evil or corrupt desire within me.

Thou, truly, art the Lord of all mankind, and the Possessor of this world and of the next. No God is there save Thee, the All-Knowing, the All-Wise.[205]

Bahá'u'lláh

EXERCISE 8
I AM CREATED TO GIVE LIFE AND LIGHT TO OTHERS

O friends! . . . Ye are the stars of the heaven of understanding, the breeze that stirreth at the break of day, the soft-flowing waters upon which must depend the very life of all men . . .

Through you We have adorned the world of being with the ornament of the knowledge of the Most Merciful. Through you the countenance of the world hath been wreathed in smiles, and the brightness of His light shone forth . . . Speed ye forth from the horizon of power, in the name of your Lord, the Unconstrained, and announce unto His servants, with wisdom and eloquence, the tidings of this Cause, whose splendour hath been shed upon the world of being.[206]

Bahá'u'lláh

The Faith of the Blessed Beauty is summoning mankind to safety and love, to amity and peace; it hath raised up its tabernacle on the heights of the earth, and directeth its call to all nations. Wherefore, O ye who are God's lovers, know ye the value of this precious Faith, obey its teachings, walk in this road that is drawn straight, and show ye this way to the people. Lift up your voices and sing out the song of the Kingdom. Spread far and wide the precepts and counsels of the loving Lord, so that this world will change into another world, and this darksome earth will be flooded with light, and the dead body of mankind will arise and live; so that every soul will ask for immortality, through the holy breaths of God.

Soon will your swiftly-passing days be over, and the fame and riches, the comforts, the joys provided by this rubbish-heap, the world, will be gone without a trace. Summon ye, then, the people to God, and invite humanity to follow the example of the Company on high . . . Think ye at all times of rendering some service to every member of the human race. Pay ye no heed to aversion and rejection, to disdain, hostility, injustice: act ye in the opposite way. Be ye sincerely kind, not in appearance only. Let each one of God's loved ones centre his attention on this: to be the Lord's mercy to men; to be the Lord's grace. Let him do some good to every person whose path he crosseth, and be of some benefit to him. Let him improve the character of each and all, and reorient the minds of men. In this way, the light of divine guidance will shine forth, and the blessings of God will cradle all mankind: for love is light, no matter in what abode it dwelleth; and hate is darkness, no matter where it may make its nest. O friends of God! That the hidden Mystery may stand revealed, and the secret essence of all things may be disclosed, strive ye to banish that darkness for ever and ever.[207]

'Abdu'l-Bahá

Suggestions for meditation every morning and evening (10–15 minutes)

1. Read carefully through all the quotations above every morning and evening during the period you work with this exercise. Select one or two sentences each time for meditation and learn them by heart. Continue for several days until you have given attention to all or most of the statements that occur in the quotations.

2. Repeat the sentences you have learnt by heart, then formulate your response to them in the form of a positive affirmation, for instance:

"God has bestowed on me the light of His holiness."

"I am able to shine with the light of God's love, and to share this light with others."

"Yes, I accept that God has given me the purpose of imparting new life to the world."

"God has inspired me to spread joy and wisdom."

"I am the servant of God and of all my fellow human beings."

"I want to give to others the greatest gift of all: the love of Bahá'u'lláh, that comes through faith in Him."

You can make your own affirmation based on the particular sentence you selected.

3. During the mornings, close your eyes, call on the Greatest Name, repeat your short affirmation and pray God to show you how you can fulfil today the purpose God has given you, and what are the services that God wants you to perform. Do not be unrealistic in setting your goals; remember that if you do even a little thing with sincerity and devotion, the Holy Spirit is capable of enlarging the effect of it infinitely, so long as what you do is in line with God's Covenant for this day.

4. During the evenings, remind yourself what were the services you decided to perform in the morning, and how you succeeded in carrying them out. If you feel you have failed, do not reproach yourself harshly, but promise yourself to do better next day. Do not let feelings of guilt build up and become the driving force for your action (or your lack of action). Your feelings of guilt will give guilt to others, and instead of sharing happiness you will share sadness. Rather let the joy, light and love that you find in the quotations above fill you, so that these energies may motivate you to act and influence every one who meets you.

5. During the day, silently repeat your affirmation as often as you can, if possible several times every hour. Whenever you have the opportunity, sit down for a couple of minutes, close your eyes, repeat your affirmation, and let your higher self think about your function in this world. When you open your eyes, look around you without selecting or avoiding any particular object and say: "This is the world to which I shall impart God's love and light. This is the purpose of my life."

6. Having said the obligatory midday prayer, sit down, dwell upon the words of the first sentence, which states why you were created, and let your higher self illumine you on the subject. Reflect on how building a new world order, inspired by God's Manifestation for this age, is a natural part of your purpose in life.

* * *

To strengthen your determination and to call upon the assistance of the Holy Spirit, use these prayers frequently and eventually learn them by heart:

Praise be to Thee, O Lord my God! I implore Thee, by Thy Name which none hath befittingly recognized, and whose import no soul hath fathomed; I beseech Thee, by Him Who is the Fountainhead of Thy Revelation and the Dayspring of Thy signs, to make my heart to be a receptacle of Thy love and of remembrance of Thee. Knit it, then, to Thy most great Ocean, that from it may flow out the living waters of Thy wisdom and the crystal streams of Thy glorification and praise.

The limbs of my body testify to Thy unity, and the hair of my head declareth the power of Thy sovereignty and might. I have stood at the door of Thy grace with utter self-effacement and complete abnegation, and clung to the hem of Thy bounty, and fixed mine eyes upon the horizon of Thy gifts.

Do thou destine for me, O my God, what becometh the greatness of Thy majesty, and assist me, by Thy strengthening grace, so to teach Thy Cause that the dead may speed out of their sepulchres, and rush forth towards Thee, trusting wholly in Thee, and fixing their gaze upon the orient of Thy Cause, and the dawning-place of Thy Revelation.

Thou, verily, art the Most Powerful, the Most High, the All-Knowing, the All-Wise.[208]

Bahá'u'lláh

O God! O God! This is a broken-winged bird and his flight is very slow – assist him so that he may fly toward the apex of prosperity and salvation, wing his way with the utmost joy and happiness throughout the illimitable space, raise his melody in Thy Supreme Name in all the regions, exhilarate the ears with this call, and brighten the eyes by beholding the signs of guidance.

O Lord! I am single, alone and lowly. For me there is no support save Thee, no helper except Thee and no sustainer beside Thee. Confirm me in Thy service, assist me with the cohorts of Thy angels, make me victorious in the promotion of Thy Word and suffer me to speak out Thy wisdom amongst Thy creatures. Verily, Thou art the helper of the weak and the defender of the little ones, and verily Thou art the Powerful, the Mighty and the Unconstrained.[209]

'Abdu'l-Bahá

BIBLIOGRAPHY

'Abdu'l-Bahá. *Paris Talks*. London: Bahá'í Publishing Trust, 1995.
— *The Promulgation of Universal Peace*. Wilmette, IL: Bahá'í Publishing Trust, 1982.
— *Selections from the Writings of 'Abdu'l-Bahá*. Haifa: Bahá'í World Centre, 1978.
— *Tablets of Abdul Baha Abbas*, Vol. 1. Chicago: Bahai Publishing Society, 1909.
— *Tablets of the Divine Plan*. Wilmette, IL: Bahá'í Publishing Trust, 1977.
— *The Will and Testament of 'Abdu'l-Bahá*. Wilmette, IL: Bahá'í Publishing Trust, 1993.
The Báb. *Selections from the Writings of the Báb*. Haifa: Bahá'í World Centre, 1976.
Bahá'í Prayers: A Selection of Prayers revealed by Bahá'u'lláh, the Báb and 'Abdu'l-Bahá. Wilmette, IL: Bahá'í Publishing Trust, 2002.
Bahá'í Prayers, A Selection. London: Bahá'í Publishing Trust, 1975.
Bahá'í World Faith. Wilmette, IL: Bahá'í Publishing Trust, 2nd edn. 1976.
Bahá'u'lláh. *Gleanings from the Writings of Bahá'u'lláh*. Wilmette, IL: Bahá'í Publishing Trust, 1983.
— *The Hidden Words*. Wilmette, IL: Bahá'í Publishing Trust, 1990.
— *The Kitáb-i-Aqdas*. Haifa: Bahá'í World Centre, 1992.
— *Prayers and Meditations*. Wilmette, IL: Bahá'í Publishing Trust, 1987.
— *The Seven Valleys and the Four Valleys*. Wilmette, IL: Bahá'í Publishing Trust, 1991.
— *The Summons of the Lord of Hosts*. Haifa: Bahá'í World Centre, 2002.
— *Tablets of Bahá'u'lláh revealed after the Kitáb-i-Aqdas*. Haifa: Bahá'í World Centre, 1978.

Compilation of Compilations, The. Prepared by the Universal House of Justice 1963–1990. 2 vols. [Sydney]: Bahá'í Publications Australia, 1991.

A Course in Miracles. Foundation for Inner Peace, 1992.

The Divine Art of Living: Selections from the Writings of Bahá'u'lláh and 'Abdu'l-Bahá. Wilmette, IL: Bahá'í Publishing Trust, 1986.

Lie, Kaare (trans.). Nyanaponika Thera, in *Oppmerksomhetstrening, kjernen i buddhistisk meditasjon.* Oslo: Solum Forlag, 1988.

Lights of Guidance: A Bahá'í Reference File. Compiled by Helen Hornby. New Delhi: Bahá'í Publishing Trust, 5th edn. 1997.

Living the Life. London: Bahá'í Publishing Trust, 1974.

Paul, Jordan and Margaret. "The Journey from Conflict to Love", in *Lotus* (Fall 1991).

Shoghi Effendi. *The Advent of Divine Justice.* Wilmette, IL: Bahá'í Publishing Trust, 1990.

— *The World Order of Bahá'u'lláh.* Wilmette, IL: Bahá'í Publishing Trust, 1991.

Star of the West. rpt. Oxford: George Ronald, 1984.

Thoresen, Lasse. *Unlocking the Gate of the Heart. Keys to Personal Transformation: A Bahá'í Approach.* Oxford: George Ronald, 1998.

Townshend, George. "A Study of a Christlike Character", *Church of Ireland Gazette* (1935), in Hofman (ed.), *'Abdu'l-Bahá, the Master.* Oxford: George Ronald, 1987.

Universal House of Justice. *Messages from the Universal House of Justice 1963–1986: The Third Epoch of the Formative Age.* Wilmette, IL: Bahá'í Publishing Trust, 1996.

REFERENCES

1. Bahá'u'lláh, *Gleanings* V: 1.
2. 'Abdu'l-Bahá, *Promulgation*, p. 397.
3. Bahá'u'lláh, Hidden Words, Arabic no. 3.
4. ibid., Arabic no. 4.
5. 'Abdu'l-Bahá, *Promulgation*, p. 255.
6. Bahá'u'lláh, *Bahá'í Prayers* (U.S. edition), p. 4.
7. Bahá'u'lláh, Hidden Words, Arabic no. 19.
8. Bahá'u'lláh, *Bahá'í Prayers* (U.S. edition), p. 36.
9. 'Abdu'l-Bahá, *Paris Talks*: "The Four Kinds of Love", para. 10 (pp. 194–5).
10. ibid. paras. 4–7 (pp. 193–4).
11. ibid. paras. 1–3 (p. 192).
12. 'Abdu'l-Bahá, *Selections*, p. 256.
13. ibid. p. 27.
14. ibid. p. 66.
15. ibid. pp. 20–21.
16. ibid. p. 27.
17. 'Abdu'l-Bahá, *Promulgation*, pp. 255–6.
18. Bahá'u'lláh, Hidden Words, Arabic no. 6.
19. Bahá'u'lláh, Súriy-i-Vafá, in *Tablets*, p. 189.
20. Bahá'u'lláh, *Gleanings* LXXXVI: 2.
21. 'Abdu'l-Bahá, *Paris Talks*: "The Four Kinds of Love", paras. 8–9 (p. 194).
22. Letter written on behalf of Shoghi Effendi, 4 October 1950, in *Living the Life*, p. 32.
23. 'Abdu'l-Bahá, *Paris Talks*: "The Universal Love", paras. 2–22 passim (pp. 25–9).
24. 'Abdu'l-Bahá, *Selections*, pp. 202–3.
25. Bahá'u'lláh, Súriy-i-Mulúk, para. 72, in *Summons*, p. 214; also

Gleanings CXIV: 15.

26. Letter written on behalf of Shoghi Effendi, 8 January 1949, in *Lights of Guidance*, no. 387.

27. 'Abdu'l-Bahá, *Selections*, p. 181.

28. 'Abdu'l-Bahá, *Promulgation*, p. 370.

29. 'Abdu'l-Bahá, *Bahá'í World Faith*, p. 364.

30. 'Abdu'l-Bahá, *Promulgation*, p. 321.

31. 'Abdu'l-Bahá, *Selections*, pp. 1–3. •

32. 'Abdu'l-Bahá, in *Star of the West*, vol. XVII, p. 348; also in *Lights of Guidance*, no. 390.

33. Letter written on behalf of Shoghi Effendi, 18 February 1954, in *Lights of Guidance*, no. 391.

34. 'Abdu'l-Bahá, *Paris Talks*: "Discourse at 'L'Alliance Spiritualiste' ", paras. 1–2 (p. 81).

35. Bahá'u'lláh, Kitáb-i-Aqdas, v. 75.

36. 'Abdu'l-Bahá, *Promulgation*, pp. 266–7.

37. ibid. pp. 190–91.

38. ibid. p. 269.

39. ibid. p. 392.

40. Bahá'u'lláh, *Seven Valleys*, pp. 17–18, 22.

41. ibid. pp. 18–22.

42. 'Abdu'l-Bahá, *Paris Talks*: "Theosophical Society, Paris", para. 9 (p. 131).

43. 'Abdu'l-Bahá, *Promulgation*, pp. 95–6.

44. ibid. p. 392.

45. ibid. p. 321.

46. 'Abdu'l-Bahá, Paris Talks: "The Eleventh Principle – The Power of the Holy Spirit", paras. 1–4, 10–13 (pp. 172–5).

47. ibid: "The Universal Love", paras. 24–6 (p. 29).

48. ibid. paras. 18–20 (p. 28).

49. 'Abdu'l-Bahá, *Promulgation*, p. 391.

50. 'Abdu'l-Bahá, *Selections*, p. 31.

51. 'Abdu'l-Bahá, *Bahá'í World Faith*, p. 364.

52. 'Abdu'l-Bahá, *Promulgation*, pp. 256–7.

53. Bahá'u'lláh, *Kitáb-i-Aqdas*, v. 148.

54. 'Abdu'l-Bahá, Will and Testament, para. 23.

55. Bahá'u'lláh, *Gleanings* V: 5.

56. 'Abdu'l-Bahá, *Bahá'í World Faith*, p. 364.

57. Bahá'u'lláh, Hidden Words, Arabic no. 5.
58. Bahá'u'lláh, Kitáb-i-Aqdas, v. 3–4.
59. Lasse Thoresen, *Unlocking the Gate of the Heart. Keys to Personal Transformation: A Bahá'í Approach.* Oxford: George Ronald, 1998.
60. Bahá'u'lláh, Aṣl-i-Kullu'l-<u>Kh</u>ayr (Words of Wisdom), in *Tablets*, p. 155.
61. Bahá'u'lláh, Hidden Words, Arabic no. 16.
62. Bahá'u'lláh, *Gleanings* CXXXVI: 2.
63. Bahá'u'lláh, *Hidden Words*, Arabic no. 8.
64. ibid. Arabic no. 40.
65. Bahá'u'lláh, in *Bahá'í Prayers: A Selection* (U.K. edition), p. 61.
66. 'Abdu'l-Bahá, Tablet of Visitation, in most Bahá'í prayer books.
67. Bahá'u'lláh, Hidden Words, Arabic no. 12.
68. ibid. Persian 29.
69. ibid. Persian no. 12.
70. 'Abdu'l-Bahá, *Selections*, p. 190.
71. 'Abdu'l-Bahá, *Promulgation*, p. 53.
72. Bahá'u'lláh, Hidden Words, Arabic no. 1.
73. ibid. Arabic no. 59.
74. ibid. Persian no. 11.
75. Bahá'u'lláh, *Prayers and Meditations*, CLIII.
76. Bahá'u'lláh, *Bahá'í Prayers* (U.S. edition), pp. 73–4.
77. Bahá'u'lláh, Hidden Words, Arabic no. 14.
78. Bahá'u'lláh, *Gleanings* CXXIII: 3–4.
79. ibid. XCIII: 5.
80. Bahá'u'llah, Hidden Words, Arabic no. 9.
81. ibid. Arabic no. 10.
82. ibid. Arabic no. 13.
83. ibid. Arabic no. 70.
84. 'Abdu'l-Bahá, *Tablets*, pp. 673–4; also in *Divine Art of Living*, pp. 29–30.
85. Bahá'u'lláh, Hidden Words, Arabic no. 36.
86. ibid. Arabic no. 34.
87. ibid. Arabic no. 11.
88. ibid. Persian no. 73.
89. Bahá'u'lláh, *Gleanings* XCVI: 3.
90. Bahá'u'lláh, quoted in Shoghi Effendi, *Advent*, pp. 75–6.

91. Bahá'u'lláh, Hidden Words, Arabic no. 51.
92. ibid. Arabic no. 48.
93. ibid. Arabic no. 50.
94. Bahá'u'lláh, *Prayers and Meditations*, CXXVII.
95. 'Abdu'l-Bahá, *Promulgation*, pp. 464–6.
96. 'Abdu'l-Bahá, *Selections*, p. 242.
97. Bahá'u'lláh, *Tablets*, p. 264.
98. 'Abdu'l-Bahá, *Selections*, pp. 257–8.
99. 'Abdu'l-Bahá, *Paris Talks*: "The Eleventh Principle – The Power of the Holy Spirit", paras. 14–15 (p. 175).
100. 'Abdu'l-Bahá, *Tablets*, p. 705; also in *Bahá'í World Faith*, p. 369.
101. 'Abdu'l-Bahá, *Bahá'í Prayers*, (U.S. edition), p. 208; also in 'Abdu'l-Bahá, *Tablets of the Divine Plan*, p. 107.
102. 'Abdu'l-Bahá, *Selections*, p. 30.
103. 'Abdu'l-Bahá, *Promulgation*, p. 96.
104. Bahá'u'lláh, Súriy-i-Mulúk, para. 63, in *Summons*, p. 211; also in *Gleanings* CXIV.
105. Shoghi Effendi, "The Unfoldment of World Civilization", in *World Order of Bahá'u'lláh*, pp. 197–8.
106. 'Abdu'l-Bahá, *Paris Talks*: "The Four Kinds of Love", para. 7 (pp. 193–4).
107. Bahá'u'lláh, Hidden Words, Arabic no. 30.
108. ibid. Arabic no. 68.
109. Letter written on behalf of Shoghi Effendi, 12 May 1925, in *Living the Life*, p. 10.
110. Bahá'u'lláh, *Gleanings* V: 4.
111. Bahá'u'lláh, quoted in a letter from the Universal House of Justice, 27 March 1978, in *Messages*, p. 376.
112. 'Abdu'l-Bahá, *Selections*, p. 63.
113. ibid. p. 292.
114. ibid. p. 169.
115. 'Abdu'l-Bahá, *Promulgation*, pp. 129–30.
116. Bahá'u'lláh, *Gleanings* CLIII: 8.
117. 'Abdu'l-Bahá, *Promulgation*, p. 93.
118. ibid. p. 129.
119. George Townshend, "Study of a Christlike Character", p. 48.
120. Letter written on behalf of Shoghi Effendi, 4 October 1950, in *Living the Life*, p. 32.

121. 'Abdu'l-Bahá, *Selections*, p. 24.

122. 'Abdu'l-Bahá, *Promulgation*, p. 267.

123. ibid. p. 453.

124. 'Abdu'l-Bahá, *Paris Talks*: "The Pitiful Causes of War . . .", paras. 7–11 (p. 19).

125. ibid: "The Universal Love", paras. 21–2 (pp. 28–9).

126. Bahá'u'lláh, Hidden Words, Persian no. 74.

127. ibid. Arabic no. 26.

128. ibid. Arabic no. 27.

129. Letter written on behalf of Shoghi Effendi, 12 May 1925, in *Living the Life*, p. 10.

130. 'Abdu'l-Bahá, in *Star of the West*, vol. IV, no. 11, p. 192; also in *Lights of Guidance*, no. 312.

131. 'Abdu'l-Bahá, *Selections*, pp. 230–31.

132. Letter written on behalf of Shoghi Effendi, 11 January 1950, in *Lights of Guidance*, no. 310.

133. Letter written on behalf of Shoghi Effendi, 30 September 1949, in *Living the Life*, pp. 30–31.

134. Letter written on behalf of Shoghi Effendi, 11 February 1925, in *Lights of Guidance*, no. 305.

135. Letter from the Universal House of Justice, 23 September 1975, in *Lights of Guidance*, no. 311.

136. Letter from the Universal House of Justice, 13 August 1980, in *Lights of Guidance*, no. 309.

137. Bahá'u'lláh, Kitáb-i-Aqdas, v. 153.

138. 'Abdu'l-Bahá, *Selections*, p. 73.

139. 'Abdu'l-Bahá, *Divine Art of Living*, p. 9.

140. Bahá'u'lláh, Súriy-i-Mulúk, para. 69, in *Summons*, p. 213; also *Gleanings* CXIV: 12.

141. Bahá'u'lláh, *Gleanings* CXLVI.

142. Bahá'u'lláh, Kitáb-i-'Ahd, in *Tablets*, p. 222.

143. 'Abdu'l-Bahá, *Selections*, pp. 21–2.

144. ibid. p. 22.

145. Letter written on behalf of Shoghi Effendi, 5 October 1950, in *Living the Life*, p. 33.

146. Bahá'u'lláh, *Gleanings* V: 3.

147. ibid. CXXXII: 5.

148. 'Abdu'l-Bahá, *Promulgation*, p. 453.

149. Letter written on behalf of Shoghi Effendi, 19 September 1948, in *Living the Life*, p. 29.

150. 'Abdu'l-Bahá, *Paris Talks*: "Beauty and harmony in diversity", paras. 8–10 (pp. 45–6).

151. 'Abdu'l-Bahá, *Selections*, pp. 2–3.

152. The Báb, Persian Bayán II: 16, *Selections from the Writings of the Báb*, p. 77.

153. 'Abdu'l-Bahá, *Selections*, pp. 1–3.

154. ibid. p. 205.

155. Letter written on behalf of Shoghi Effendi, 5 December 1942, in *Lights of Guidance*, no. 1345.

156. 'Abdu'l-Bahá, *Selections*, p. 277.

157. 'Abdu'l-Bahá, *Tablets of the Divine Plan*, p. 56.

158. Letter written on behalf of Shoghi Effendi, 18 March 1950, in *Lights of Guidance*, no. 1340.

159. Letter written on behalf of Shoghi Effendi, 4 October 1950, ibid. no. 1344.

160. Letter written on behalf of Shoghi Effendi, 16 February 1951, in *Living the Life*, pp. 33–4.

161. 'Abdu'l-Bahá, in *Compilation*, vol. I, no. 934.

162. ibid. no. 933.

163. Letter written on behalf of Shoghi Effendi, 26 October 1943, in *Compilation*, vol. II, no. 1469.

164. Message from the Universal House of Justice to the Bahá'ís of the World, September 1964, in *Messages*, no. 19.

165. Letter written on behalf of Shoghi Effendi, 18 March 1950, in *Lights of Guidance*, no. 1340.

166. 'Abdu'l-Bahá, *Bahá'í World Faith*, pp. 359–60.

167. 'Abdu'l-Bahá, *Promulgation*, p. 169.

168. 'Abdu'l-Bahá, *Selections*, p. 36.

169. Bahá'u'lláh, Kitáb-i-Aqdas, v. 18.

170. 'Abdu'l-Bahá, *Tablets*, p. 706; also in *Bahá'í World Faith*, p. 369.

171. Bahá'u'lláh, Hidden Words, Arabic no.16.

172. ibid. Arabic no. 59.

173. Bahá'u'lláh, *Gleanings* CXXXVI: 5–6.

174. 'Abdu'l-Bahá, *Selections*, pp. 202–3.

175. Letter written on behalf of Shoghi Effendi, 31 January 1949, in *Compilation*, vol. II, no. 1779.

176. Bahá'u'lláh, *Prayers and Meditations* XCVI.
177. Bahá'u'lláh, *Hidden Words*, Arabic no. 36.
178. ibid. Persian no. 12.
179. Bahá'u'lláh, *Gleanings* XXVII: 2.
180. ibid. CXXXVI: 5
181. Bahá'u'lláh, Hidden Words, Arabic no. 13.
182. ibid. Arabic no. 12.
183. ibid. Arabic no. 14.
184. ibid. Arabic no. 11.
185. ibid. Arabic no. 9.
186. ibid. Arabic no. 10.
187. ibid. Persian no. 31.
188. ibid. Persian no. 44.
189. Shoghi Effendi, "The Unfoldment of World Civilization", in *World Order of Bahá'u'lláh*, pp. 197–8.
190. 'Abdu'l-Bahá, *Promulgation*, p. 93.
191. 'Abdu'l-Bahá, *Selections*, p. 169.
192. ibid. p. 24.
193. 'Abdu'l-Bahá, *Paris Talks*: "The Four Kinds of Love", para. 7 (pp. 193–4).
194. Bahá'u'lláh, Hidden Words, Arabic no. 51.
195. ibid. no. 48.
196. ibid. no. 49.
197. 'Abdu'l-Bahá, *Paris Talks*: "Pain and Sorrow", para. 3 (p. 110).
198. Bahá'u'lláh, Gleanings CXXIII: 3–4.
199. 'Abdu'l-Bahá, quoted in a letter from the Universal House of Justice, 13 August 1980, in *Lights of Guidance*, no. 309.
200. Bahá'u'lláh, *Gleanings* CXLVI.
201. 'Abdu'l-Bahá, in *The Divine Art of Living*, p. 9.
202. Bahá'u'lláh, Kitáb-i-'Ahd, in *Tablets*, p. 222.
203. Bahá'u'lláh, *Prayers and Meditations* CXXVII.
204. Bahá'u'lláh, The Four Valleys, p. 58; The Seven Valleys, pp. 9, 8, 9.
205. Bahá'u'lláh, *Bahá'í Prayers* (U.S. edition), p. 48.
206. Bahá'u'lláh, excerpts compiled and arranged by Shoghi Effendi, *The Advent of Divine Justice*, pp. 75–6. Shoghi Effendi comments: " . . . these immortal passages . . . cannot fail to produce on the minds and hearts of any one . . . who

approaches them with befitting humility and detachment, such powerful reactions as to illuminate his entire being and intensify tremendously his daily exertions."

207. 'Abdu'l-Bahá, *Selections*, pp. 2–3.
208. Bahá'u'lláh, *Bahá'í Prayers* (U.S. edition), pp. 195–6.
209. 'Abdu'l-Bahá, ibid. pp. 216–7.